A PRION GUIDE

LONDON HOTELS

of character, distinction & charm

A PRION GUIDE

LONDON HOTELS

of character, distinction
& charm

Nina Prommer and Rosalyn Singer

PRION

First published in the United Kingdom 1992 by
PRION,
an imprint of Multimedia Books Limited,
32 – 34 Gordon House Road, London NW5 1LP

Editor   Linda Sonntag
Editorial assistant   Anna Kirby
Project editor   Anne Cope
Design and maps   Kelly j Maskall
Photography   Brian Cohen, Neill Menneer
Production   Hugh Allan
Picture research   Nina Prommer, Rosalyn Singer,
     Charlotte Deane

British Library Cataloguing-in-Publication Data
Prommer, Nina
     London hotels of character, distinction and charm
     I. Title II. Singer, Rosalyn
     647.94421

     ISBN   1-85375-098-0

Printed in Italy by New Interlitho

CONTENTS

Key to price symbols

Singles

£	£39 - 75
££	£75 - 105
£££	£105 - 150
££££	£150 - 280 or more

Doubles

£	£49 - 90
££	£90 - 130
£££	£130 - 180
££££	£180 - 280 or more

Suites, studios, apartments

£	£80 - 130
££	£130 - 205
£££	£205 - 250
££££	£250 - 500 or more

As seasoned travellers, both on business and for pleasure, we have stayed in many fine hotels throughout the world. Our experience of hotels in London, on our own territory, was comparatively limited. It was not until our jobs required us to book hotels in the capital for visitors from abroad that we realized the need for a guide devoted exclusively to the kind of London hotels we found they liked best: hotels of character, distinction and charm.

In researching this book we looked at location, décor and value for money, friendliness, efficiency and cleanliness. Excellence in all these categories allowed us to include a wide range of hotels. Besides the many discreet 'boutique' hotels that offer the best in comfort, luxury and personal service, we discovered many surprises, including a two-bedroomed hotel in a private house, a floating hotel on the River Thames, and a newly built airport hotel with over 500 rooms.

All the hotels in this book are unique and highly recommended. But not all of them are super-luxurious, because we genuinely wanted to portray a range of hotels to suit a range of pockets and a range of tastes. London has many hotels with more than adequate amenities, in good locations, at reasonable prices.

We have not specified tariffs, since these date quickly, but we have indicated price bands for each hotel (see price symbols opposite). You are advised to check with the hotel at the time of booking for current rates.

One of the most pleasing discoveries that we made during our researches was that most hotels with an in-house restaurant have very reasonably priced menus. For hotels without restaurants, we recommend where to eat nearby. Some hotels also have lively bars, which are often open to non-residents; others have no bar at all. In those without a bar, guests are provided with a mini bar in their rooms or, in some cases, a fridge which they can fill with drinks themselves.

For those using public transport, we have made a note of the nearest tube stations and convenient bus routes (please note that the latter are subject to change).

The 70+ hotels in this book are our own personal choice; we hope they will give you as much pleasure as they have given us.

Ros Singer and Nina Prommer

Mayfair St James's Soho

This area is bordered on the north by Oxford Street, on the east by the Charing Cross Road, on the south by St James's Park and Green Park, and on the west by Hyde Park.

Mayfair today is the home of wealth and elegance. Here the visitor will find expensive shops, luxury hotels and casinos. But this area was not always so select. It takes its name from an annual fair that had to be suppressed by George II in 1800 because of the riotous behaviour of its stallholders and revellers.

The area was established in around 1700, and within a century had been laid out in squares and terraces. The largest is Grosvenor Square. It has lost its original houses, and the United States Embassy now stands at its western end, but original houses remain on the south side of the oldest square, Hanover Square. Berkeley Square, famous for the fact that a nightingale is supposed to have sung there, has magnificent 200-year-old plane trees.

The best and most exclusive shopping, for clothes and antiques, is to be found in and around Bond Street, with particularly fashionable boutiques in South Molton Street. Just north of Piccadilly at the Hyde Park Corner end is Shepherd Market, Mayfair's "village", with alleys full of smart shops, cafés and restaurants.

• • • • • • • • • •

St James's is an area south of Regent Street, bordered by Green Park and Pall Mall. This is where the true English gentleman may be seen walking to his club or shopping for snuff or made-to-measure shirts. In 1665 this land was granted by the king to the Earl of St Albans in acknowledgement of his loyalty. Its close proximity to Buckingham Palace ensured that property here would be highly desirable, and the earl began building at once.

Pall Mall is lined with gentlemen's clubs, as is St James's Street, which leads through to Piccadilly. Here you can find the Conservative drinking club White's, Boodles, which was a gambling haunt of Beau Brummell in Regency times, Brooks' and the Carlton.

Jermyn Street and Savile Row are the two most prestigious streets in London for gentlemen to shop in. In Jermyn Street you can buy moustache wax and traditional shaving brushes at Trumpers, and a meerschaum pipe at Astleys. The best shirts in town are to be had at Harvie and Hudson or Turnbull and Asser, while headwear may be purchased at James Lock or Bates. In Savile Row, H. Huntsman and Sons specialize, appropriately

Left: A view of Whitehall from St James's Park.

Below: Military customers emerging from Gieves & Hawkes, Savile Row.

enough, in riding clothes, and have been patronized by royalty for over a century. Other famous clothiers here are Gieves & Hawkes, Anderson & Sheppard and Tommy Nutter. If antiques are more your line, Christie's auction house is right in the middle of St James's in King Street.

Soho lies in the heart of the West End, with its boundaries along Oxford Street, Regent Street, Shaftesbury Avenue and the Charing Cross Road. Soho is famous for its cosmopolitan character, its nightlife, restaurants and delicatessens, and for being the hub of the sex industry in London. In the south, Soho spills over Shaftesbury Avenue into Chinatown, with its excellent restaurants and markets. In the rest of Soho, the flavours are predominantly Italian, Greek and French. People come here to buy food as well as to eat it, and open-air Berwick Street market is famous for its fresh exotic produce, as well as for fruit and vegetables brought in from the home counties. Ronnie Scott's is a well known jazz venue, and visitors may

also want to stroll down Carnaby Street, though this pedestrianized thoroughfare has lost much of its sixties' excitement.

Above: Shop windows in Oxford Street.

Left: The temptations of a Soho patisserie.

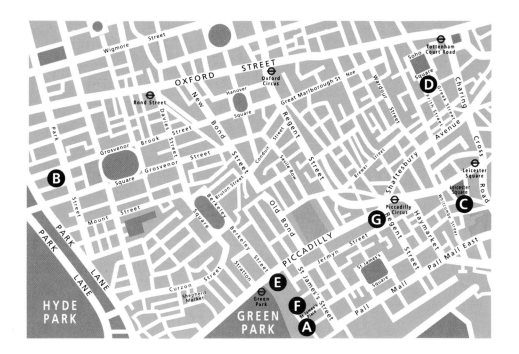

A Dukes Hotel

B Fortyseven Park Street

C The Hampshire

D Hazlitt's

E The Ritz

F The Stafford

G 22 Jermyn Street

⊖ London Underground

Dukes Hotel

St James's Place London SW1A 1NY
Tel 071 491 4840 Fax 071 493 1264 Telex 28283

38 rooms and 26 suites with bath and shower, telephone, tv with teletext, radio, ceiling fan, hairdryer, bathrobes • 24-hour room service, English and Continental breakfast, laundry, dry cleaning • business services, conference room, safe, air-conditioning in public areas • in-house restaurant with imaginative modern cuisine • limited parking • no animals • single room ££££, double room ££££, suite ££££, excluding breakfast, all major credit cards • tube: Green Park; bus nos: 9, 14, 22, 25, 38

Situated in a small cul-de-sac off St James's, Dukes opened as a hotel in 1908 and has recently been rebuilt and refurbished. Its original aim was to retain the ambience of a private residence, and it succeeds in doing so to this day.

Entry to the hotel is through a picturesque flower-filled courtyard, where gas lamps are lit by hand every evening. The spacious lobby leads to a small and distinctive panelled bar with oil paintings and leather tub chairs. The bar has the

•••••••••

seasoned atmosphere of an old-fashioned gentlemen's club. Its speciality is vintage cognac and the service is impeccable and unobtrusive.

The bedrooms have been enlarged and the bathrooms finished in marble. The bedrooms are individually designed and feature fine classic furnishings, luxurious king-size and four-poster beds and deep comfortable sofas. Thoughtful touches in the guest rooms include complimentary bottled mineral water, hairdryers, plush towelling on heated towel rails, bathrobes and personal toiletries by Floris. Some rooms have open fires, and there are wooden colonial-style fans overhead.

Some suites have a kitchenette, room service is excellent, and guests can also enjoy the intimate and award-winning restaurant. The wines have been carefully selected and the manager describes the cuisine as "creative modern English." The dining room is quintessentially English, decorated with trompe l'oeil paintings and softly lit at night. Guests can also take morning coffee, afternoon tea and cocktails in the cosy sitting room.

The Marlborough Suite can accommodate up to 50 people for a banquet or twice that number for cocktails, and there are other private dining facilities for business and social occasions. Dukes is nothing if not elegant, and house rules require that gentlemen wear a jacket and tie: jeans and training shoes will not do.

An outstanding venue for a private party is Dukes Penthouse Suite, which has a roof terrace with a spectacular view over London's West End. The management invites guests to sample cocktails and canapés in this unique setting every few weeks.

Another special service offered by the hotel is the preparation of a traditional picnic basket, which can be enjoyed a few minutes' walk away in the tranquil surroundings of Green Park or St James's Park.

Guests return to their rooms at night to find the beds turned down and nightclothes laid out ready, another sign of the attention paid to small details in this elegant and comfortable hotel.

Fortyseven Park Street

47 Park Street London W1Y 4EB
Tel 071 491 7282 Fax 071 491 7281 Telex 22116 LUXURY
Toll free USA 1 800 451 5536; France 19 05 90 84 74; Sweden 020 795160;
Canada 1 800 463 6061

52 air-conditioned suites with bath and shower, telephone, personal fax,
satellite tv with CNN, in-house movies, video, radio, bar, full kitchen
facilities, hairdryer, bathrobes, scales, safe • 24-hour room service, hot and
cold snacks, English and Continental breakfast, laundry, dry cleaning, valet
service • business services, conference rooms • in-house restaurant:
Le Gavroche, open Monday to Friday • meter parking, car valet •
no animals • suite ££££, breakfast not included, all major credits cards and
En Route • tube: Marble Arch; bus nos: 2B, 12, 16, 88, 137

Built in 1926 in the heart of Mayfair by the first Baron Milford, this beautiful hotel
with its impressive columned façade is only a block away from the US Embassy
and a short walk from Hyde Park and fashionable Bond Street. Under the umbrella
of Relais & Château, it combines the only Michelin three-star restaurant in
London, run by Albert Roux, with luxury accommodation that consists solely of

• • • • • • • • • •

one- or two-bedroomed suites.

Albert Roux is a legendary figure in the culinary world, and whether you decide to eat in the famous restaurant or order from room service, you are in for the gourmet experience of a lifetime.

We arrived on a baking hot day. The doorman took care of our car and luggage and we were shown without fuss to our air-conditioned suite, where a bottle of chilled champagne awaited us. The spacious lounge was tastefully furnished with a comfortable sofa and armchairs in a delicate floral print, a huge desk and a dining table for six. Two display cabinets held books and china, which guests may purchase as souvenirs of their stay. We admired the elegant panelled walls, the corniced ceiling, and the stunning display of potted plants. The centrepiece of the room was an ornamental fireplace in carved wood and marble with a large gilded overmantel mirror.

Our bedroom had plenty of wardrobe space, crisp white duvets and a large dressing table. The woodwork was in yew. The suite had two marble bathrooms with scales, the most generous supply of Floris toiletries and soft towelling robes. Each suite has its own beautifully equipped kitchen. The staff will even do the

shopping for guests who want to cook, but we decided to take advantage of room service after joining management and other guests for cocktails and delicious canapés in the newly refurbished oak-panelled lounge.

Breakfast en suite was a delightful experience. It arrived swiftly. A waiter deftly set our table and announced: "Ladies, your breakfast is served!" We really enjoyed the warm croissants and brioches, which had been freshly baked on the premises.

The Hampshire

Leicester Square London WC2H 7LH
Tel 071 839 9399 Fax 071 930 8122 Telex 914848

124 air-conditioned rooms with bath and shower, telephone, satellite tv
with Sky, CNN and in-house movies, radio, mini bar (no teasmade),
bathrobes, trouserpress, hairdryer, slippers, mints • 24-hour room service,
hot and cold snacks, English and Continental breakfast, laundry, dry
cleaning • business services, safe, 4 conference rooms • in-house restaurants:
Oscars, Celebrities • lift, meter parking, valet • animals welcome
by arrangement • single room ££££, double room ££££, suite ££££,
breakfast not included, all major credit cards, including JCB and
En Route • tube: Leicester Square; bus nos: 1, 3, 6, 9, 11, 12, 13, 53, 88

This elegant red-brick building with its wrought iron and canopied neo-classical
entrance on the south side of Leicester Square is an oasis of luxury. Within two
years of opening, the hotel had been voted one of the top five new business hotels

• • • • • • • • • •

in the world by *Business Traveller Magazine.*

In the reception and bar we found rich mahogany panelling, rose of aurora marble and deep handmade carpets. The owner has travelled extensively in the Far East and brought back beautiful carpets and and pots, which we noticed throughout the hotel.

There is a small intimate drawing room, traditionally furnished in the country house style. In front of a fire in the magnificent marble fireplace you can enjoy thin cucumber sandwiches or a Devonshire cream tea.

The hotel has three main colour schemes for its bedrooms – deep blue, peach and burgundy – but the four-poster rooms and the suites are individually decorated. The furniture is in satinwood and rosewood, and even the less expensive rooms are lavishly furnished and of a good size.

We stayed in one of the enormous studio rooms. Here we found a romantic canopied bed, a basket of gorgeous dried flowers, and a huge writing desk that doubles as a dressing table. The Hampshire's bathrooms are among the very best in town. They are finished in Sicilian marble, have twin washbasins, a separate shower and a bathtub with yet another powerful shower behind glass panels. There was also a separate toilet.

The hotel has a choice of restaurants. In the basement is a bistro-style wine bar called Oscars, and on the ground floor is a formal dining room, Celebrities. Oscars, with its wooden floors and bare stone walls, is quite unique. Alcoves for intimate dining are named after showbusiness personalities such as Monroe, Olivier and Valentino, and on some evenings there is live entertainment from singers or pianists. Oscars is open to non-residents and stays open late. Celebrities also has a theatrical theme. The food here is French and there is an excellent wine list.

Business travellers will appreciate the stylish and sophisticated conference

facilities, and the banqueting suite on the top floor with its spectacular views of Trafalgar Square and the Houses of Parliament. There is also a business centre with secretarial services if required.

Hazlitt's

6 Frith Street London W1V 5TZ
Tel 071 434 1771 Fax 071 439 1524

23 rooms, 22 with bath, one with shower; telephone, tv (no radio), hairdryer, iron on request (no mini bar or teasmade) • laundry, dry cleaning, Continental breakfast served in your room • business services, safe, no conference room • nearest restaurants: Alastair Little, L'Hippocampe, La Capannina • no lift or parking • no animals • single room ££, double room ££, suite £££, breakfast not included, all major credit cards • tube: Leicester Square, Tottenham Court Road; bus nos: 10, 14, 19, 24, 25, 38, 73

This hotel is unique in many ways. It occupies three townhouses in Frith Street and has not changed much in character since it was built in 1718. It is named after William Hazlitt, poet, journalist, historian and philosopher, who died there in 1830. The 23 rooms are named after other illustrious eighteenth- and early nineteenth-century occupants or visitors to the house, among them Charles Lamb

• • • • • • • • • •

and Jonathan Swift.

In reception we were handed our keys and a front door key – reception is manned only between 7.30 a.m. and 11.30 p.m. Behind the reception is a minute sitting room, with two old-fashioned green sofas, a working fireplace, an antique chest that serves as a coffee table, a little writing desk in one corner and sepia prints and photographs on the walls.

The walls are plainly painted throughout and covered in antique prints – Hazlitt's has no wallpaper, no chintz, no frills or flounces, and neither is it ashamed of its pipework. There is not a trouserpress, a bathrobe or a teasmade in sight. The original wooden floors have settled, so in most of the rooms it's an uphill walk to bed, and doors do not fit as once they did. The original Victorian brass telephone mixer taps are inclined to drip. There are sloping linoleum-covered staircases; no elevators, no breakfast room or bar.

However, Hazlitt's has a devoted clientèle comprised of people who would find staying in the average London hotel a suffocating experience.

We descended the creaking staircase to view the Thomas Archer room. In the corridor outside we admired an unusual wall clock, and were told it was used for clocking Victorian workers in and out. Inside we found antique pine furniture, a washstand with ewer and jug, an alcove with a pretty display of porcelain, and an illuminated bust set amid green plants.

We stayed in the Baron Willoughby suite. Its marble fireplace had been turned into a home for green plants, there was a display cabinet full of objets d'art and,

on the top of the wardrobe, a large bust of Beethoven. Prints decorated the walls and the *pièce de résistance* was a magnificent four-poster bed. The only modern object in sight was the television.

The bathrooms throughout the hotel are very individual, with original Victorian free-standing baths and mahogany toilet seats and towel rails.

The Ritz

Piccadilly London W1V 9DG
Tel 071 493 8181 Fax 071 493 2687 Telex 267200

129 rooms, mostly air-conditioned, with bath and shower, telephone,
satellite tv, video, video library, radio, mini bar, teasmade on request,
hairdryer, bathrobes • 24-hour room service, hot and cold snacks,
English and Continental breakfast, laundry, dry cleaning, valet
service • business services, 2 conference rooms, safe • in-house restaurant
with French and English cuisine • lift, NCP and meter parking •
no animals except guide dogs • single room ££££, double room ££££,
suite ££££, breakfast not included, all major credit cards •
tube: Green Park; bus nos: 14, 22, 25, 38

The Ritz is in Piccadilly, possibly the best location in London, with its entrance in
Arlington Street. Green Park is just around the corner and from there you can
stroll to Buckingham Palace. Also nearby are the finest shopping streets in London,
the Royal Academy and London's theatreland.

To enter the Ritz is to step inside a world of grandeur created by its founder

• • • • • • • • • •

César Ritz, and opened in 1906. Anyone in blue jeans and sneakers will be politely turned away, but it is a pleasure to dress for the part and enjoy the tradition of The Ritz, with its impeccable service that yet has an air of informality and friendliness.

The public areas on the ground floor are an invitation to participate in the high life of the Edwardian era, its frivolity and elegance. The timeless custom of afternoon tea can be enjoyed in the Palm Court with its gilded statuary, exuberant fountain and Louis XIV armchairs. As the rose-filtered natural light fades, two gilded wrought iron lanterns are lit at dusk on Fridays and Saturdays in readiness for an after-theatre dance to the Big Band sound of the Twenties, Thirties and Forties. We needed little encouragement to join in the celebrations and found it a uniquely thrilling experience.

The Ritz Restaurant is reached via the elegant Long Gallery. There is much to enjoy in this magnificent room, in addition to the famous haute cuisine of the Ritz and its award-winning wine list. We marvelled at the painted ceiling, the chandeliers and the walls of different marbles.

Even the smallest bedrooms are a good size by anyone's standards. The suites and rooms are decorated in the opulent style of Louis XVI and feature large modern marbled bathrooms with gold fittings to echo the gilt trimmings in the bedrooms. We loved the marble fireplaces, the statuary, and the beautiful ornate

clocks we found everywhere. We found the delicate pastels of our Belle Epoque surroundings restful and soothing after a hectic day out.

The rich and famous from all over the world are regular visitors at The Ritz, still the place to come for inimitable luxury combined with the finest traditions of hotel-keeping.

· · · · · · · · ·

The Stafford

St James's Place London SW1A 1NJ
Tel 071 493 0111 Fax 071 493 7121 Telex 28602 STAFRD G

74 rooms with bath and shower and fan or air-conditioning, tv with CNN, radio, bathrobes, slippers, hairdryer on request, safe • 24-hour room service, hot and cold snacks, English and Continental breakfast, laundry, dry cleaning • business services, 4 conference rooms • in-house restaurant serving French cuisine • lift, parking on request • no animals • single room £££££, double room £££££, suite £££££, not including breakfast, all major credit cards • tube: Green Park; bus nos: 9, 14, 19, 22, 25, 38

The dining room in the 350-year-old stone wine cellars of The Stafford must be one of London's best kept secrets. This cellar is said to have housed the wines from nearby St James's Palace before becoming part of the hotel. Around 800 labels and 20,000 bottles of the finest wines are stored here, and the sommelier will take bottles out of stock on request, so you can make sure your favourite vintage is waiting for you on your next visit to the hotel. The crystal, silver and starched linen on the cellar table provide a romantic contrast with the starkness of the vaulted room, which makes a lovely venue for a candlelit dinner for up to 30 people. Management will also arrange wine tastings for up to 75 guests.

Instead of staying in the main building, we opted for a suite in the new

Carriage House. Built on land adjoining the hotel in the eighteenth century, this was originally a stables, and overlooks a delightful cobbled courtyard. Our room had a pitched ceiling with exposed beams, and we noticed many authentic touches, right down to the ground floor doors, designed like real stable doors.

The colour scheme was forest green and butter yellow, and the furnishings mostly antique, though we noticed some handmade pieces in natural beech, burnished with beeswax. There was a fireplace, a comfortable sofa and wing chairs, and a magnificent four-poster bed. Equestrian paintings on the wall added the perfect finishing touch. An extraordinary feature of our room was a stereo system with a CD player and a CD selection: a real luxury. In the main building the bedrooms are decorated with mahogany, chintz and crisp Irish linen.

The hotel is famous for its American Bar, and for Charles, the barman, who has been with The Stafford for over 30 years. We found he mixed a mean martini. In the eighteenth century The Stafford was a club, and the atmosphere and the impeccable service hark back to those days. Every inch of the bar's ceiling is covered in ties, caps and sports memorabilia given to Charles by the hotel's guests, and the black cat Whiskey dozes on a chair that he has made his own. A light lunch may be taken in the bar, or guests may eat in the restaurant, where the menu features such unusual British specialities as seagull eggs and wild oysters from Scotland, available for only a few days each year.

The head porter at The Stafford has a particular welcome for the hotel's many regular visitors, who are often astonished at his remarkable memory for names and faces as he enquires after their families. He is the best person to consult on the historic neighbourhood of the hotel, as well as on where to shop in St James's.

22 Jermyn Street

London SW1Y 6HL
Tel 071 734 2353 Fax 071 734 0750

13 suites and five studios with bath and shower, telephone in all rooms and bathrooms, private incoming direct line on request, fax, 10-channel television with movie channel, teletext, CNN, radio, mini bar, hairdryer, bathrobes, air conditioning on request • 24-hour room service, hot and cold snacks, Continental and English breakfast, laundry, dry cleaning • business services, safe, conference rooms in suite for 12 people • nearest restaurants: Wiltons, Suntory, Le Caprice • lift, valet parking • no animals • single room £££, double room £££, suite £££–££££, not including breakfast, all major credit cards • tube: Piccadilly; bus nos: 9, 12, 14, 15, 19, 22, 38, 88, 159

In 1915 the owner's grandfather bought this building and established residential chambers. In 1939 his father took over the business and when he recently wanted to sell, the present owner was ready for action. He bought the hotel from his father, even though he had no previous involvement in the hotel business apart from his personal experience of staying in first-rate hotels all over the world.

   With the help of his wife Suzanne, an innovative interior designer, Henry Togna completely transformed the hotel into the remarkable establishment it is today. It is very refreshing to find every facility a large five-star hotel would offer, but without the impersonality of many chains.

Inside the unobtrusive front door, a long narrow foyer leads to a small reception desk, which is dominated by an amazing flower arrangement. There are 13 suites and five studios, but no public lounge or dining room. Instead the room service menu offers gourmet delicacies and an excellent wine list, and is available at all hours for private dining or entertaining in the suites.

Our suite was a very good size, the burgundy curtains in the sitting room voluptuously draped, the striped sofa and armchairs soft and inviting. Architectural prints and well chosen antiques are a welcome change from frills. There was a large mirror over the original Edwardian fireplace that gave the room a touch of home. An abundance of fresh flowers and plants showed lavish attention to detail, and we were impressed to find two personal telephone lines and a private fax.

The bedroom with its king size bed had an antique dressing table, and the sofa in the lounge converts to an extra bed, should this be needed. There was a well stocked bookshelf, and ardent readers can pick up the phone and ask for reception to contact nearby Hatchards, should they not find a title to their fancy. The book will be delivered immediately and charged to the hotel account.

The bathroom was stunning. Here we found dark grey granite instead of marble, well lit mirrors, and radio speakers for those who enjoy music while soaking in a fragrant bath.

Among its special services, such as 24-hour medical and dental care, the hotel offers access to a de luxe health club with swimming pool, squash courts, gymnasium and exercise classes.

The location is excellent: Jermyn Street is famous the world over for bowler hats, cashmere coats, handmade shirts, tweed jackets, moustache wax, custom-made shoes and the finest cigars. The Haymarket Theatre, the Royal Academy,

Bond Street and tea at Fortnum & Mason's are all nearby.

Sophisticated travellers will really appreciate the outstanding individual service offered at this hotel: room service is even happy to supply bread for the ducks in St James's Park.

Bloomsbury, Marylebone

South of Regents Park runs the Marylebone Road, which, east of the park, changes its name to the Euston Road. The district of Marylebone lies in the west of this section of the map below this great thoroughfare, while Bloomsbury lies to the east.

Bloomsbury has a reputation for being London's most important literary "village". In the early years of this century a number of literary and artistic figures made it their home, and they came to be known as the Bloomsbury Group. Its leading lights included Virginia and Leonard Woolf, Roger Fry, Lytton Strachey and Maynard Keynes. They were known not only for their artistic achievements, but also for their liberal morals, and they made a flamboyant contrast with the previous Victorian generation. Other artistic figures who were not members of the Group were attracted by the refreshingly progressive atmosphere in Bloomsbury, and T.S. Eliot, Bertrand Russell and D.H. Lawrence came to live there too.

Today Bloomsbury is the home of many publishing houses, and its academic status is permanently assured by the presence of London University and the British Museum.

Bloomsbury is an area of fine Georgian squares. In 1660 the Earl of Southampton built a palace for himself in Bloomsbury Square, but nothing of the original building has survived, though there is a lovely garden. Bedford Square, built in 1775, is virtually intact. It is London's finest square, with terraces of dark brick houses with stuccoed, pedimented centres surrounding a beautiful private garden. South of Russell Square, with its magnificent plane trees, is an enclave of charming narrow streets around Museum Street packed with second-hand and antiquarian bookshops.

In Gower Street is University College, built in the classical style in 1827-9. It stands well back from the road and has an imposing dome and portico. The university buildings are scattered throughout this area, with Senate House, the London University Library, in Malet Street, and the University Church of Christ the King in Gordon Square.

British Telecom Tower, still called by its old name of the Post Office Tower, soars above the area at 619 feet. It was built in 1964 to improve broadcasting reception over the surrounding tall buildings, and is no longer open to the public.

The name Marylebone comes from St Mary-le-bourne, or Mary by the brook. This elegantly laid out area extends south from Regents Park towards Oxford Street, and consists mainly of smart residences. The names of some of its streets will be immediately familiar to the visitor. Here you

will find Baker Street, home of Sir Arthur Conan Doyle's detective Sherlock Holmes; Wimpole Street, home of the Barrett family, whose daughter Elizabeth married Robert Browning; and Harley Street, lined with the practices and consulting rooms of Britain's top private doctors and dentists.

Hertford House in Manchester Square houses the Wallace Collection, the finest collection of French art to be found outside

Far left: Marylebone Road with Regents Park in the background.

Left: Covent Garden Market.

France. Two of London's top tourist attractions, Madame Tussaud's and the Planetarium, are to be found in the Marylebone Road, a minute away from Baker Street station.

Madame Tussaud began wax modelling in her native France, where she worked to immortalize great historical figures both before and during the French Revolution (models of some of those who were beheaded can be seen in the Chamber of Horrors). She came to England in 1802 and founded her waxworks museum in London in 1837. New models are constantly added to the collection: Mikhail Gorbachev, Joan Collins, and Luciano Pavarotti are among the latest.

The Planetarium next door, with its striking green copper dome, stages spectacular "starshows" on astronomy. In the evening, the Laserium offers a rock music and laser extravaganza.

Above: The imposing bulk of the British Museum.

Right: Pollock's Toy Museum, Charlotte Street, W1.

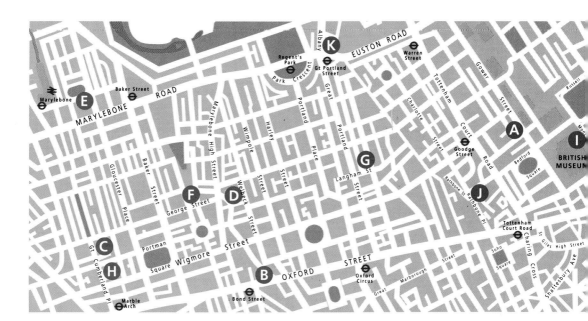

A The Academy Hotel

B The Berkshire Hotel

C Bryanston Court Hotel

D The Clifton-Ford

E Dorset Square Hotel

F Durrants Hotel

G The Langham Court Hotel

H The Montcalm

I The Portland Bloomsbury

J The Rathbone Hotel

K The White House

London Underground

British Rail

The Academy Hotel

17-21 Gower Street London WC1E 6HG
Tel 071 631 4115 Fax 071 636 3442 Telex 24364
Toll free USA only 1 800 678 3096

33 rooms, 25 with bath and shower, all with telephone, tv, radio, teasmade, hairdryers and air conditioning in studio suites, ironing board on request • 24-hour room service, hot and cold snacks, no mini bar, Continental, English or à la carte breakfast, laundry, dry cleaning • business services, safe, no conference room • in-house restaurant: GHQ • NCP and meter parking • no animals • single room £–££, double room £–££, suite ££, excluding breakfast, all major credit cards • tube: Tottenham Court Road; bus nos: 7, 8, 10, 14, 19, 22, 24, 25, 29, 38, 55, 73, 503

• • • • • • • • • •

This elegant Georgian hotel is situated in the heart of Bloomsbury, once London's literary quarter, centred around the home of Virginia Woolf. The Academy Hotel is within easy walking distance of the British Museum, the library of London University at Senate House, fashionable Covent Garden and the theatres of the West End. The three townhouses that comprise the hotel are double-glazed to the front to ensure a peaceful night.

Behind the classical façade is a modern reception and lounge with the original fireplace, in stunning azure blue, carefully preserved. At the back of the building

Bloomsbury bluestockings can find sanctuary in the library. This delightful room with its pale blue and peach décor gives on to a secluded patio. Residents can be served lunch or afternoon tea on the patio, and on hot summer nights enjoy informal suppers.

The peach and blue theme extends to the tastefully furnished rooms, where it mingles with sunny yellow. Fresh flowers and potted plants bring the colour scheme to life. The generous American-size beds have brilliant white duvets. There are two air-conditioned deluxe studio suites, which are particularly imaginatively furnished. We stayed in a room with a four-poster bed and a comfortable deep-cushioned sofa. All the rooms have plenty of cupboard space.

All but eight of the rooms have their own bathrooms, which are finished in marble and well equipped with heated towel rails and large mirrors. A graded tariff reflects the snug or spacious nature of the accommodation.

The Academy Hotel's restaurant, GHQ, is a gourmets' delight, with a small imaginative menu offering organic vegetables, and herbs grown on the premises. Both dining rooms are modern in design, featuring mellow wood and emerald upholstered dining chairs. There is air conditioning and the tables are well spaced to allow for private conversation.

GHQ offers non-residents a club membership with various entitlements, such as a birthday lunch or dinner on the house. Open until the early hours, it is an ideal place for after-theatre dining, and you can occasionally listen to live jazz in the GHQ bar.

The Berkshire Hotel

350 Oxford Street London W1N OBY
Tel 071 897 6644 Fax 071 759 8422 Telex 22270

**147 air-conditioned rooms with bath and shower, telephone, satellite
and cable tv with CNN and in-house movies, radio, mini bar (no teasmade)
trouserpress, hairdryer, bathrobes, scales in suites • 24-hour room service,
hot and cold snacks, English and Continental breakfast, laundry,
dry cleaning • business services, safe, 2 conference rooms • in-house
restaurant: Ascots • lift, NCP and meter parking • animals welcome by
arrangement • single room ££££, double room ££££, suite ££££, breakfast
not included, all major credit cards, including JCB and En Route •
tube: Bond Street; bus nos: 6, 7, 8, 12, 13, 25, 503**

The Berkshire enjoys a very central location in Oxford Street, but once inside,
it's difficult to believe that you are in the heart of the West End, because the
ambience is that of a typical English country house. The Berkshire was voted Hotel
of the Year in the 1989 Catey Awards, and won the prestigious RAC Blue
Ribbon in 1990.

The drawing room is opposite the reception and here we found a working
fireplace flanked by bookcases. We noticed handsome green plants in Chinese pots,

• • • • • • • • • •

antique lace on glass table tops and fragrant pot pourri.

On the first floor in Ascots Bar is one of the best barmen in town. He will make you any cocktail you care to drink and even invent one to your own inspiration. The bar is wood-panelled and hung with racing prints. We sat in comfortable tub chairs to drink our cocktails. Of course the racing theme runs through to the award-winning restaurant, Ascots, next door. Here we found a unique feature: a calorie-counted menu for weight-conscious diners.

The hotel has 147 rooms and there are two entire no-smoking floors. The suites are individually decorated and very spacious. The Sunningdale Suite was decorated in yellow, pink and blue, with a mahogany dining table and chairs. Its bathroom was finished in grey and pink marble with gold fittings. In it we found a jacuzzi bathtub and a bidet, bathrobes, slippers, and a telephone extension.

Elsewhere in the hotel we saw beautiful silk rugs from India, Pakistan and China, and objets d'art from many parts of the world. The whole hotel is air-conditioned, with individual controls in each bedroom.

The Berkshire offers a late supper tray, which may be ordered before leaving the hotel for the evening. There are two menus, and the tray will be brought to your room at any time between 11.30 p.m. and 4.30 a.m. The pre-theatre dinner includes a chauffeur-driven car to the theatre. Business visitors can make use of the splendid conference rooms, one of which has an adjoining double bedroom.

The Berkshire's staff are obliging and friendly, and made our stay a very pleasant one indeed.

Bryanston Court Hotel

56-60 Great Cumberland Place London W1H 0DD
Tel 071 262 3141 Fax 071 262 7248 Telex 262076

54 rooms with bath or shower, telephone, cable tv, radio, teasmade (no
mini bar), hairdryer • room service with cold snacks from 4.00 to 9.30 p.m,
English and Continental breakfast, laundry, dry cleaning • business
services, safe, conference room • nearest restaurants: Stephen Bull's,
Biagi's • lift, NCP and meter parking, 2 private spaces • animals welcome
by arrangement • single room £, double room £, including
Continental breakfast, all major credit cards • tube: Marble Arch;
bus nos: 6, 7, 8, 12, 16, 74

The Bryanston Court is an Edwardian hotel conveniently located one minute's
walk from Marble Arch and Oxford Street. The building was occupied by the
American War Office during World War II. Attractive blue canopies and wrought
iron balconies distinguish the façade. A black and white tiled forecourt leads to the
reception. The staff were friendly and check-in procedures swift: our luggage was
taken up to our room while we explored the public areas.

The sitting room is decorated in peach with leather button-backed chesterfields
and armchairs, which give it the feel of an old-fashioned club. We noticed green
plants, oil paintings, interesting knick-knacks in a display cabinet, dried flowers
and Austrian blinds. In the bar at the back of the building, entertainment comes by

● ● ● ● ● ● ● ● ●

courtesy of an invisible piano player, who gives recitals on disc. The bar is wood-panelled, dimly lit and informal in atmosphere.

The bedrooms are uniformly furnished and decorated. The emphasis here is on simplicity, and we found clean uncluttered lines and a refreshing absence of frills, flounces and swags. The bathrooms are all en suite, some have baths and others showers, but all are modern and well equipped with toiletries.

There is no restaurant in this hotel, but the central location means that there is a wide choice of places to eat nearby. Breakfast is served downstairs, and Continental breakfast is included in the very reasonable tariff, though a full English breakfast may be ordered for a small extra charge.

What we liked about this hotel was its comfortable simplicity, efficient service, good amenities and very reasonable price for such a central location.

The Clifton Ford

Welbeck Street London W1M 8DN
Tel 071 486 6600 Fax 071 486 7492 Telex 22569

200 rooms with bath and shower, air conditioning on two floors, telephone, tv, video, radio, mini bar, teasmade, hairdryer, trouserpress, bathrobes, scales • 24-hour room service, hot and cold snacks, buffet and English breakfast, laundry, dry cleaning • business services, safe, 8 conference rooms • in-house restaurant with English cuisine • lift, parking for 20 cars • animals welcome on request • single room £££–££££, double room £££–££££, suite £££–££££, breakfast not included, all major credit cards • tube: Bond Street; bus nos: 6, 7, 8, 10, 12, 94, 137, 503

Johan Osmael Scott-Ellis, the ninth Baron Howard de Walden, is the landlord of the estate on which this hotel stands. His ancestor, Lord Thomas Howard, the first Baron de Walden, was summoned to Parliament in 1597 to become Earl Marshal of England, and was largely responsible for uncovering Guy Fawkes's dastardly gunpowder plot in 1605.

This privately owned hotel started life as a lodging house for gentlewomen in 1866. It is situated in the heart of Marylebone village. The hotel has a modern façade, but once we stepped through the door, which is flanked with bay trees, the

• • • • • • • • • •

mood changed. The grand entrance area leads to a comfortable lounge decorated and furnished in the classical English style. The colour scheme is warm soft peach and cream, and there are graceful arches and stuccoed pillars and panelling. In one alcove is a white grand piano, which is played in the evening for the guests' entertainment. The bar is panelled in dark wood, in the style of a gentlemen's club.

In the friendly dining room, we inspected the menu. The choice was extensive, with typically English fare as well as a selection of international dishes. We were particularly impressed by the unusual choices offered for breakfast, such as hot waffles, steak and eggs, and gravad lax.

We were taken to the top of the hotel to admire the fabulous Penthouse Suite. This has a private curved staircase hung with a crystal chandelier, and an unrivalled view across the rooftops of London. The windows extend the length of the drawing room wall, and there is a wonderful display of flowers and green plants in the window boxes and tumbling over the elaborate wrought-iron balustrade on the private terrace outside. The Penthouse Suite is decorated in peach and black, and beautifully furnished with fine quality oriental antiques, including Chinese cabinets, sumptuously complemented by rich fabrics and Chinese rugs.

Each floor has a different colour scheme. Yew is used in the green rooms, the blue rooms gleam with polished brass, and the gold rooms are enriched with satinwood and specially commissioned tapestries. The gold rooms also have striking black and white tiger-striped marble bathrooms.

The Clifton-Ford has the most up-to-date and high-tech conference facilities, and business travellers are offered a wide range of special services.

Dorset Square Hotel

39-40 Dorset Square London NW1 6QN
Tel 071 723 7874 Fax 071 724 3328 Telex 263964 DORSET G
Toll free USA 1 800 5434138

37 rooms, 28 with bath, 9 with shower; air conditioning, telephone,
satellite tv, radio, mini bar, hot-water bottles, bathrobes, hairdryer, curling
tongs • 24-hour room service, hot and cold snacks, English and Continental
breakfast, laundry, dry cleaning, valet, shoe cleaning • business services,
safe, conference room • in-house restaurant • lift,
NCP and meter parking, chauffeur-driven Bentley on request •
no animals • single room ££, double room ££–£££, suite £££, not including
breakfast, all major credit cards except Diners • tube: Baker Street;
bus nos: 2B, 13, 74, 159, 349

This hotel, in a restored Regency building, overlooks two acres of tree-filled
gardens in Dorset Square, the site of Thomas Lord's first cricket ground. The
connection with cricket is evident throughout the hotel: the porters are dressed in
cricket sweaters; in the entrance hall we noticed cricket bats signed by famous

• • • • • • • • • •

players in a wrought-iron umbrella stand; and cricket prints and memorabilia are displayed throughout the hotel.

The richly elegant reception and sitting room has a large mahogany desk and a working marble fireplace with an ornately carved wooden mantel. Unusually delicate arrangements of fresh flowers and blue and white Chinese porcelain are reflected in a gilt-framed mirror, and a display cabinet holds interesting memorabilia that are offered for sale.

In the drawing room we found an honesty bar tucked away in an antique cabinet and a nineteenth-century roll-top desk packed with stationery for the use of guests. Everywhere there were interesting touches.

The bedrooms are delightfully decorated: we saw richly striped walls and generous swags of floral fabric, and admired the owner's bold talent for combining colour and pattern to stunning effect. We noticed oil paintings, marble busts, candelabra constructed from crystal chandeliers, French armoires and antique lace.

We stayed in a beautiful room decorated in pink and green, with a comfortable coronet bed and ample hanging space in the mirrored wardrobe. The grey marble bathroom had good lighting and mirrors, old-fashioned fittings, bathroom scales and plenty of toiletries.

Downstairs the restaurant walls are decorated with murals depicting scenes from Regents Park and Dorset Square, and the furnishings suggest a very elegant farmhouse kitchen. In the bar a chessboard waits on a pine table, and china is

attractively displayed on a large Welsh dresser. Guests are entertained to live classical music on Tuesday evenings, and live jazz on Thursdays.

An additional benefit of staying in this charming hotel is use of the private gardens in the square; a chauffeur-driven Bentley Continental is also at guests' disposal.

Durrants Hotel

George Street London W1H 6BJ
Tel 071 935 8131 Fax 071 487 3510 Telex 814919 DURHOT

**96 rooms, 80 with bath, 6 with shower, 10 without facilities, telephone, tv,
radio, mini bars in suites, hairdryer, complimetary mineral water • 24-hour
room service, English and Continental breakfast (English breakfast
in the breakfast room only), laundry, dry cleaning • business services,
conference rooms, safe, no air-conditioning • in-house restaurant with
French and English cuisine • lift, meter parking • no animals • single
room ££, double room ££, suite ££, breakfast not included,
all major credit cards except Diners • tube: Bond Street, Baker Street;
bus nos: 2B, 10, 13, 74, 159, 349**

Originally a seventeenth-century coaching inn, with stables built on at the back,
this is the oldest privately owned hotel in London, having been in the same family
for the last 70 years.

The hotel has a distinguished Georgian façade, which is decorated in summer
with box upon box of cheerful geraniums. The George Bar has a working fireplace,
antique pine furniture and muskets displayed on the walls, and offers a most
interesting and extensive selection of Scotch whisky. The lounge, which used to be

the owner's office, is beautifully panelled in oak, hung with oil paintings, and furnished with leather armchairs.

The restaurant also gives the feeling of a gentlemen's club. The mahogany booths and leather banquettes ensure privacy, and the discreet and considerate service enables even the solitary diner to feel at home. We can thoroughly recommend the English fare from the silver trolley; other dishes may be chosen from the à la carte menu.

For private dining, the Armfield Room, named after the artist whose oils hang on the pine-panelled walls, is one of three banqueting rooms that may be booked for business or social occasions. Conference facilities cater for up to 50 guests for lunch and dinner, and 120 guests for meetings and wedding receptions.

A sweeping mahogany staircase leads to the bedrooms. All but 10 of the rooms have en suite baths or showers, and at the top end of the price range are family rooms and de luxe suites. The furniture is traditional, with some limed oak as well as mahogany, as befits a family hotel. The smaller, quieter rooms are at the back.

The bathrooms have been refurbished in pale grey marble. Guests in the very reasonably priced rooms without facilities have a separate bathroom across the corridor. Suites have mini bars.

The service is dignified and hospitable, and throughout the hotel we enjoyed an old-world charm that seemed far removed from the bustle of central London.

The Langham Court Hotel

31-35 Langham Street London W1N 5RE
Tel 071 436 6622 Fax 071 436 2303 Telex 21331

56 rooms, 42 with bath, 14 with shower, telephone, tv, radio, hairdryer,
trouserpress (no mini bar) • 24-hour room service, hot and cold snacks,
English and Continental breakfast, laundry, dry cleaning • business
services, conference room, safe • in-house restaurant: Langham's
Brasserie, and Vino Latinos tapas bar • lift, NCP parking • animals
welcome by prior arrangement • single room ££, double room ££,
breakfast not included, all major credit cards • tube: Oxford Circus;
bus nos: C2, 3, 6, 7, 8, 10, 12, 73, 135

• • • • • • • • • •

Built in 1899 as an elegant private townhouse, The Langham Court Hotel is situated in a quiet street within easy walking distance of the West End in a part of London dominated by broadcasting and the fashion industry. The striking black and white glazed brick façade has been restored to its original splendour and there is a beautiful ornately carved entrance arch. This listed building has a twin in Amsterdam with exactly the same distinctive frontage.

The interior has also been scrupulously restored to incorporate all the amenities expected by the modern international traveller. The restful blue lounge with its burnt orange sofas has rosewood furniture imported from China and highly decorative Chinese vases. The architectural prints on the walls tell their own story.

Langham's Brasserie at the back of the hotel serves good French food. The wooden floor and marbled peach walls give the room an elegant Continental look. Here we ate Velouté de volaille, a tasty chicken soup; followed by Truite bretonne, trout with prawns and mushrooms; and cheese from a huge selection. On the breakfast menu we found baked beans, smoked haddock and black pudding as well as the more predictable Continental breakfast.

Vino Latinos is The Langham Court's more informal wine bar, where tapas are served. The wooden floor, long wooden bar, high glass-topped tables and bar stools reminded us of Mediterranean holidays. An area at the back has skylight windows and round tables with tub chairs, and must be a perfect place to unwind at lunchtime or in the evening after a busy day.

We took the lift from the black and green marble foyer to inspect the bedrooms. These are uniform in décor. Wardrobes and headboards are of ash with

maple insets, and there are pink and blue floral curtains and matching bedspreads. The bathrooms are of Italian marble and very well equipped. Some rooms have showers only.

For business visitors the hotel offers full secretarial services and a large conference room called the Titchfield Suite, which is also used for promotions, exibitions and dinner dances.

The Montcalm

Great Cumberland Place London W1A 2LF
Tel 071 402 4288 Fax 071 742 9180 Telex 28710

115 air-conditioned rooms with bath and shower, telephone, satellite tv
with CNN, radio, mini bar, bathrobes, hairdryer, duvets on request •
24-hour room service, hot and cold snacks, English, Continental and
Japanese breakfast, laundry, dry cleaning • business services, safe,
2 conference rooms • in-house restaurant: Les Célébrités • lift,
NCP parking • animals welcome by arrangement • single room ££££,
double room ££££, suite ££££, breakfast not included, all major credit
cards • tube: Marble Arch; bus nos: 6, 7, 8, 10, 12, 16, 36, 137

• • • • • • • • • •

A friendly porter took care of our luggage as we stepped through the polished door into the grand foyer of the Montcalm with its restful décor and antique furniture. We noticed in particular a beautiful old French writing bureau. The scent of flowers filled the air.

The accommodation here includes 12 unique duplex apartments and two penthouse suites, which offer additional space and luxury. The duplexes have two entrances: one to enter the sitting room, and one on the floor above to enter the bedroom, so that private meetings need not be disturbed. All the rooms are air-conditioned and tastefully furnished in soft muted colours with some leather chairs. The bathrooms have well lit mirrors and toothbrushes are provided among the usual toiletries.

We took a drink in the bar before dinner and found the barman to be a very amusing character, full of anecdotes and helpful shopping tips. He told us about Bermondsey market, where bargain hunters arrive at dawn each Friday to get first pick, but we were not so keen to miss out on a luxurious lie-in.

The Montcalm's restaurant, Les Célébrités, is elegantly decorated in pink and burgundy, and the pink damask on the tables and the pink Austrian blinds give a luxurious and intimate atmosphere to the dining area. We admired the bronze sculptures and were told that the contemporary paintings on the wall are for sale. The inspiration behind the food is French. Lunch at the Montcalm is particularly good value as it includes unlimited house wine with a set three-course meal.

The Montcalm offers special weekend breaks, which include full traditional English breakfast, valet car parking, a bottle of chilled champagne on arrival and a daily newspaper.

The Portland Bloomsbury

7 Montague Street London WC1B 5BP
Tel 071 323 1717 Fax 071 636 6499

27 rooms, 25 with bath, 2 with shower; telephone, satellite tv, radio,
hairdryer, trouserpress, mineral water, chocolates (no mini bar or
teasmade) • 24-hour room service, hot and cold snacks, English and
Continental breakfast, laundry, dry cleaning • business services, safe,
conference room for 15 people • in-house Italian restaurant • lift,
meter parking • no animals • single room ££, double room ££, suite ££,
including breakfast, all major credit cards • tube: Russell Square;
bus nos: 8, 19, 22, 38, 55, 68, 188, 503

This handsome Regency townhouse is situated in the heart of Bloomsbury just off
Russell Square. Refurbished in May 1990 to a very high standard, the hotel is
decorated in the country house style. An elegant marble-floored entrance leads to
the reception, with a lift to the four floors. The reception is bright and airy with
pretty floral curtains and plenty of fresh flowers. Beyond it is a small tastefully
furnished sitting room. The paintings and antiques, not to mention piles of

• • • • • • • • • •

magazines and periodicals, make guests feel at home. The main feature of this room is a splendid fireplace in black marble and brick with an antique pine overmantel.

The bedrooms are individually decorated in keeping with the period of the building. Most rooms were spacious, and we noticed furniture in walnut and floral fabrics, though our favourite room was decorated entirely in blue and green tartan, which made an interesting change from pastels. All the en suite bathrooms were finished in pink marble and were well equipped with toiletries. There was a

different colour scheme for the corridors on each floor – we noticed coffee, blue and gold – so even the most absentminded of guests could not get lost.

Some of the rooms at the back of the building overlook the pretty patio garden, which backs on to the British Museum. Weather permitting, breakfast, lunch, tea or dinner can be taken in this secluded garden, which is an oasis of peace and tranquillity. The rooms at the back of the hotel are also extremely quiet, two streets away from any traffic.

Downstairs in the bar the atmosphere is relaxed. The rich green walls are hung with pictures and the bar stools and banquettes are covered in an exotic jungle print.

The adjoining restaurant is open all day and offers a wide selection of dishes. The cuisine is Italian, and besides a good choice of pasta there is simply grilled fish and meat and, to follow, a variety of delicious desserts. The wine list is well balanced and sensibly priced. The walls of the dining room are ragged in bright yellow, which gives the effect of being constantly bathed in sunlight, and the yellow table linen provides a fresh background for the beautifully presented food.

The staff are friendly and obliging, and will arrange theatre tickets or visits to places of special interest, or simply carry a chair into the garden for you.

No guest at this hotel should neglect visiting the British Museum, for which it is so conveniently placed.

The Rathbone Hotel

Rathbone Street London W1P 1AJ
Tel 071 636 2001 Fax 071 636 3882 Telex 28728

72 air-conditioned and double-glazed rooms with bath and/or shower, telephone, satellite tv with in-house movies, radio, fridge, hairdryer, trouserpress • 24-hour room service, cold snacks round the clock, hot snacks until 11.30 p.m., English, Continental and executive breakfast, laundry, dry cleaning • business services, conference rooms, safe • in-house restaurant: The Peacock • lift, meter and NCP parking • no animals • single room ££, double room ££, suite ££, not including breakfast, all major credit cards • tube: Goodge Street; bus nos: 10, 14, 24, 38

This hotel is situated in an area of the West End known as Fitzrovia, which for the first half of the twentieth century was the home of Bohemian society. Today the creative spirit lives on in Fitzrovia, named after the nearby Fitzroy Tavern, in the form of film, television and advertising companies. Around the corner is Charlotte Street, with its many cosmopolitan restaurants; Soho and Chinatown are also close by; and the shops of Oxford Street and Regent Street are just a short walk away.

The façade of The Rathbone is modern, but the atmosphere inside is surprisingly personal. We admired the marble floor and the striking deep blue

• • • • • • • • •

oriental carpet, the warm rosewood panelling, chandeliers and huge Chinese urns. Among the antiques and objets d'art we noticed a beautiful French bureau.

The Peacock Bar on the ground floor is also rosewood-panelled, the colours are warm and soft, and the sofas comfortable. The bar's specialities are cocktails such as Opal Hush and Kir Royale, which we sampled before going up to our room.

An elevator took us to our floor. The fifth floor has thoughtfully been reserved for non-smokers. All the bedrooms were refurbished and double-glazed in 1991. The good-sized bed in our room had a wood-panelled headboard draped in silk, and the furnishings were in subtle shades of terracotta. Gazing up at the ceiling we were amused to discover a lightly painted sky with a cherub peeping from the cornice. Beautiful Italian standard lamps and a selection of prints on the wall put the finishing touches to this elegant room.

The bathrooms are of warm pink marble, and in the executive rooms and suites whirlpool baths and body massage showers promise relaxation after a busy day.

In the Peacock Restaurant, with its coral and cream décor, the chef creates delicate and elegantly presented dishes. The menu is predominantly French.

The staff are friendly and helpful, and one of the services we found particularly useful is the in-house travel agency. Here you can order a bodyguard, charter a private plane or book a helicopter ride. The Rathbone also prides itself on getting tickets for the most popular shows, even when they are declared to be sold out.

Although the hotel is very central, we were charmed by the colourful village atmosphere that still thrives in Fitzrovia.

The White House

Albany Street London NW1 3UP
Tel 071 387 1200 Fax 071 388 0091 Telex 24111

576 rooms with bath and shower (some air conditioning), telephone,
satellite tv with movie channel and teletext, radio, mini bar, hairdryer,
trouserpress, double glazing, some no-smoking rooms • 24-hour room
service, hot and cold snacks, English and Continental breakfast, laundry,
dry cleaning • business services, 7 conference rooms, safe • fitness centre •
café, 2 bars, wine bar and restaurant in house • 4 lifts, limited free
parking, NCP • animals welcome by arrangement • single room ££–£££,
double room ££–£££, suite ££–££££, breakfast not included, all major
credit cards • tube: Great Portland Street; bus nos: A2, C2, 135, 349

This unique building, set on an island between Albany Street and Osnaburgh
Street, started out in 1936 as a block of luxury flats. There were 758 apartments,
furnished or unfurnished, with or without service. The design incorporated an
imposing entrance hall from which a lounge led to the restaurant, swimming pool
and squash courts. The basement was entirely taken up with kitchens and stores.

• • • • • • • • • •

Other areas open to non-residents included a bar, delicatessen, newsagent, chemist, hairdresser, valet and dry cleaners, and the roof doubled as a garden.

This unusual concept meant that The White House lent itself ideally to conversion into a hotel, but the process was a gentle one, as there were still many permanent residents, and took place over a 14-year period from 1959. The 1980s saw further refurbishment, and today's hotel has an award-winning French restaurant, bars, cocktail lounge, The Wine Press and The Garden Café, a fitness and sauna centre, and extensive business and banqueting facilities.

The Reserve Club on the top floor is a hotel within a hotel. With its own manager and check-in desk, it has 54 rooms including suites and studios, all equipped to the very highest standards demanded by the senior international business executive. Quite often junior executives stay in the same hotel a few floors below: a mutually convenient arrangement. In the Club Lounge, Reserve guests can enjoy complimentary tea, coffee, fresh fruit and fruit juices while browsing through the newspapers, or play chess or other board games. Room service on the Reserve floor offers a more extensive menu than on the hotel's lower floors.

The list of services offered at The White House is impressive: a doctor is on 24-hour call, and full invalid services are available, including toilet and hydraulic ramp. Management offers everything from baby sitters to mobile phones, heated rollers and feather-free pillows, and languages spoken include Arabic, French,

German, Italian, Filipino, Portuguese, Spanish and Thai.

The décor in The White House is restrained and simple, with the accent on comfort rather than opulence. The chief appeal of the hotel lies in its comprehensive range of facilities and services, which make it a world in itself.

Bayswater

The Bayswater Road is a major thoroughfare (the A40) that leads from Notting Hill Gate, along the north side of Kensington Gardens and Hyde Park, to Marble Arch. The district of Bayswater is a strip of land north of this road, bordered on the east by the Edgware Road and to the west by Pembridge Villas. To the north lie Westbourne Grove and Paddington.

The first tramway in London ran along the Bayswater Road from Marble Arch in 1861. The famous people who made their home in this area at one time or another include Edith Sitwell, who wrote *Façade* at her home at 22 Pembridge Mansions; Max Beerbohm, author and caricaturist; Wyndham Lewis, artist and author; Sir James Barrie, creator of Peter Pan; and Lord Baden-Powell, founder of the Boy Scouts.

The London Toy and Model Museum is to be found at 21 Craven Hill. This is open from Tuesday to Sunday, and it appeals as much to adults as to children. Room upon room is crammed with nursery toys, mechanical toys and a splendid collection of model railways. Many of the toys can be operated by visitors, and there is a miniature railway to ride on.

A favourite pastime for visitors in this area is to stroll along the Bayswater Road on a Sunday morning, for between Lancaster Gate and Queensway there is a weekly open-air market. Here you can find paintings for all tastes and all pockets, large oils in gilded frames and small unframed watercolours. Some of the traders come from all over Britain with examples of arts and crafts; one pitch is held by a gallery from St Ives in Cornwall.

• • • • • • • • •

Marble Arch is one of London's most famous landmarks. John Nash built it in 1828 as the entrance to Buckingham Palace, but it was moved to its present site in 1851 when Queen Victoria had the palace enlarged. It was modelled on the Arch of Constantine in Rome and was originally much more magnificent than the structure we see today surrounded by a sea of traffic. At this site once stood Tyburn Tree, London's traditional execution place from the Middle Ages until 1783. A plaque shows exactly where the gallows stood, and where large crowds gathered to watch death sentences being carried out.

Left: Business as usual at Speaker's Corner, at the Marble Arch end of the Bayswater Road.

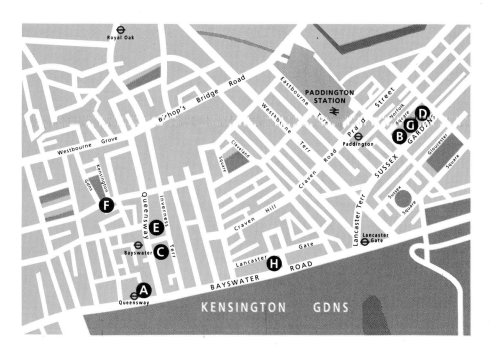

A The Coburg

B The Delmere Hotel

C The Eden Park Hotel

D The Gresham Hotel

E The Hyde Park Towers Hotel

F The Phoenix Hotel

G Royal Cambridge Hotel

H Whites Hotel

London Underground

British Rail

The Coburg

129 Bayswater Road London W2 4RJ
Tel 071 221 2217 Fax 071 229 0557 Telex 268235

132 en suite rooms with safe, colonial fan, telephone, satellite tv (no radio), hairdryer, iron, trouserpress, teasmade and biscuits, mini bar • English and Continental breakfast, laundry, dry cleaning, complimentary newspapers • business services, conference room, air conditioning in public areas • in-house restaurant: The Spice Merchant • lifts, NCP and meter parking • no animals • single room ££, double room ££–£££, suite £££, including breakfast, all major credit cards • tube: Queensway; bus nos: 12, 94

Outlined at night in fairy lights and looking like a smaller version of Harrods, this stylish Edwardian property stands on the north side of Kensington Gardens. It was built as a hotel in 1905, the fourth year of the short reign of Edward VII of the house of Saxe-Coburg, by the entrepreneur John Cuthbert Ellison. In 1990 the hotel underwent extensive refurbishment and restoration and an external face-lift.

The Coburg is known for its comfort and calm spaciousness. The large lounge bar retains its original fireplace and other architectural features, and the lobby has

• • • • • • • • • •

a handsome gallery. The traditional décor is warm and discreet, with wood panelling, brass rails and planters, and soft green and coral carpets and upholstery.

The bedrooms follow the house colour scheme, and the bathrooms are finished in Edwardian tiles, which makes a refreshing change to ubiquitous marble. The most luxurious accommodation is in the penthouse in The Coburg's dome: the Dome suite is often reserved by honeymoon couples. Its elegant bedroom has a private staircase leading up to a sumptuously furnished lounge. The suite offers panoramic views across the park. From its windows you can spot the Broad Walk, a straight tarmac avenue running from the hotel to the southern end of Kensington Gardens. It was constructed to serve as an emergency wartime runway, should the royal family have needed to escape from nearby Kensington Palace.

The Coburg's in-house restaurant is The Spice Merchant, one of London's top Indian restaurants, which also offers a number of East African dishes. The diner walks past an interesting mural depicting the interior of a spice merchant's house to a dining area that is both modern and sophisticated. Part of the kitchen has been integrated into the design, so that guests can watch the chefs at work. The spices are ground freshly every day and there is a large selection of vegetarian dishes.

Just around the corner from The Coburg is Queensway, a lively cosmopolitan thoroughfare that offers late night shopping and a selection of ethnic restaurants. Queensway Ice Skating Rink beckons to the adventurous.

The Delmere Hotel

130 Sussex Gardens London W12 1UB
Tel 071 706 3344 Fax 071 262 1863 Telex 8953857

40 rooms, 34 with shower, 6 with bath; telephone, tv, radio, teasmade (no
mini bar), hairdryer, jacuzzi (extra charge) • room service with snacks,
Continental breakfast, laundry, dry cleaning • business services, safe,
air conditioning in public areas • in-house restaurant: La Perla, with
Italian and French cuisine • lift, limited parking • animals welcome
by arrangement • single room £, double room £, including breakfast,
all major credit cards • tube: Paddington; bus nos: 7, 15, 36

• • • • • • • • • •

This stucco townhouse in tree-lined Sussex Gardens has a colonnaded entrance in the Regency style. We were welcomed in the marble-floored reception area by friendly staff and ascended by a most unusual double-entranced lift to our room.

The rooms vary in size, though the décor is similar. Each has an electronic key card for added security. Our room was furnished with large and comfortable beds and easy chairs in peach to match the curtains. Refreshment trays made a welcome addition, so we could make tea without ringing for room service.

Our room had bath and shower, and we appreciated the shower doors, which are so much more hygienic than curtains. Some rooms have jacuzzi baths, very soothing for tense muscles after a hard day.

The owner invited us to take coffee with him in the lounge and explained that he thought the personal touch all- important in a small hotel like The Delmere. He said the emphasis was on good service, and that staff quickly got to know guests by name and not just by their room number. His policy obviously works, because The Delmere has recently been awarded a certificate of distinction from the British Tourist Authority.

The lounge is a gracious room carpeted and furnished in blue and peach, with a library full of interesting books. There is a wood-panelled fireplace, and a fire is lit in winter so that guests feel as if they are in their own sitting room at home.

Visiting the hotel's restaurant, La Perla, we discovered an interesting menu dominated by Italian dishes. We noticed old favourites like spaghetti bolognese, but decided to try the chicken speciality, which came with a delicious sauce. In addition to the à la carte, there is a daily set menu with four courses. The dining room is pleasantly decorated in soft pastels and has an adjoining bar, which is ideal for pre-dinner drinks.

The Eden Park Hotel

35-39 Inverness Terrace London W2 3JS
Tel 071 221 2220 Fax 071 221 2286 Telex 263266

**137 rooms with bath and shower, telephone, satellite tv, radio, teasmade
(no mini bar), hairdryer, trouserpress • 24-hour room service, hot and cold
snacks, English and Continental breakfast, laundry, dry cleaning • business
services, safe, no conference rooms, air conditioning in public areas •
in-house restaurant: Park Brasserie • lift, meter parking • no animals,
guide dogs welcome on request • single room ££, double room ££,
breakfast not included, all major credit cards •
tube: Bayswater; bus nos: 12, 70, 94**

This hotel was built in 1860 and is situated in a quiet residential street in
Bayswater. It has recently undergone extensive refurbishment and meets the high
standards required by the modern international traveller, though the atmosphere
is still distinctly Victorian.

Walking into the foyer, we were struck by the decorative marble floor and the
frieze running around the cornice. The walls are dark red and hung with eye-
catching prints. Other features that we noticed were green plants in copper pots,
the wood-panelled reception desk, a comfortable seating area, and piped music.

The Tulip Bar has the atmosphere of a gentlemen's club. Here we found deep

• • • • • • • • • •

rich colours, paisley curtains, buttoned banquettes and mahogany tables on wrought-iron plinths. The room is dominated by a magnificent fireplace with a richly carved mantel and a large gilt-framed mirror. The bar offers a wide selection of beers, wines and spirits.

From the bar we entered the King's Restaurant, which is similarly furnished and serves traditional English food in keeping with the atmosphere. The menu changes with the seasons. A carving trolley offers a selection of roasts, and makes dining here as popular with family parties as it is with business people.

The bedrooms are similarly decorated, and vary only in size. Our room was finished in pink and blue, had a comfortable seating area and good full-length mirrors. The wardrobes were very spacious. The rooms are well appointed, with

direct-dial telephones, television with satellite channels, radio, tea and coffee making facilities, a hairdryer and a trouserpress. The bathrooms are tiled in pink, modern and well equipped. There are good supplies of fluffy towels and toiletries.

The hotel is close to two underground stations and well served by bus routes. The trip to the West End takes only a matter of minutes.

The Gresham Hotel

116 Sussex Gardens London W2 1UA
Tel 071 402 2920 Fax 071 402 3137

38 rooms, 35 with shower, 3 with bath, telephone, tv with satellite, CNN, alarm, radio, safe, teasmade, hairdryer; trouserpress and iron on request, no air conditioning • room service until midnight (no mini bar), English and Continental breakfast, laundry, dry cleaning • business services, conference room • nearest restaurant: San Marino • lift, 3 parking spaces • no animals • single room £, double room £, including full English breakfast, all major credit cards • tube: Lancaster Gate, Paddington Station, Bayswater Road, Edgware Road, Marble Arch; bus nos: 15, 27, 36

Sir Thomas Gresham founded the Royal Exchange. He laid the foundation stone in 1566 and the building was opened by Queen Elizabeth I four years later. Until this date, London's merchants had met to do business in the open air. Sir Thomas's crest bears a grasshopper. Legend has it that he was a foundling baby whose life

• • • • • • • • • •

was saved by the chirping of this insect. This charming story is apocryphal, but a grasshopper still sits on top of the Royal Exchange to remind us of its founder.

The Gresham Hotel, which also has a grasshopper incorporated in its crest, is situated in a tree-lined one-way street. Its owners, who have a wealth of experience in the hotel industry, have redeveloped and redesigned it with an impeccable eye for detail. We found it a stylish and comfortable place to stay, with friendly and welcoming service.

The bedrooms have been decorated to the highest standards, and a harmonious range of colours and quality fabrics has been chosen for each floor. Our room had pale yellow rag-rolled wallpaper and a bedspread of blue and buttercup yellow. Behind the ornate swags and pelmets was a dark blue blind: we could sleep late without being disturbed by the sun. Hand-coloured prints and house plants were further personal touches. We also noticed an antique Italian writing bureau in the reception area and an unusual wrought-iron duck doorstop.

The bar is panelled in light oak and the green-varnished, high-backed wooden bar stools are a distinctive touch. The bar leads on to a small cosy lounge. Breakfast, which is included in the hotel's very reasonable tariff, may be taken in the bright and cheerful dining room.

The Gresham Hotel offers an oasis of calm close to the heart of London. The business traveller will find it convenient for the main line station at Paddington, which serves Wales and the west of England, as well as for the M40, M4 and M1.

The Hyde Park Towers Hotel

41-51 Inverness Terrace London W2 3JN
Tel 071 221 8484 Fax 071 221 2286 Telex 263260 G

115 rooms with bath and shower, telephone, satellite tv, radio, teasmade (no mini bar), hairdryer, trouserpress • 24-hour room service, hot and cold snacks, English and Continental breakfast, laundry, dry cleaning • business services, safe, 3 conference rooms, air conditioning in public areas • in-house restaurant: Le Parc • lift, meter parking • no animals except guide dogs • single room ££, double room ££, suite ££££, not including breakfast, all major credit cards • tube: Bayswater; bus nos: 12, 94

This hotel is situated in Inverness Terrace in Bayswater, and very close to Kensington Gardens and Hyde Park. It was totally refurbished in 1990. Guests staying at this elegant hotel can enjoy the quiet surroundings of this mostly residential area while only one minute's walk from busy and lively Queensway around the corner.

  We entered the foyer with its cool marble floor and magnificent crystal chandelier

• • • • • • • • • •

and were greeted by the friendly receptionist. The foyer is beautifully panelled in yew. There is also a comfortable seating area, with plants in large Chinese urns, Indian prints, an exquisite Tiffany lamp with a flamingo base, and piped music.

The reception leads on to the cosy wood-panelled bar with its comfortable seating. We gazed up to find the whole scene reflected in the mirrored ceiling. A further door leads to Le Parc, the hotel's in-house restaurant. The cuisine here is French, and the table d'hôte menu changes daily. Cane chairs and crisp white linen give this room an elegant air, and in the morning it doubles up as the breakfast room. Our Continental breakfast was served buffet-style with an imaginative array of foods from which to choose, including salami, smoked turkey and ham.

The bedrooms are uniformly furnished and decorated. The theme here is deep blue trimmed with dark red, with comfortable tub chairs and good full-length mirrors. The bathrooms are modern, well equipped and tiled in light grey. Some are quite small, but all have ample supplies of towels and toiletries.

The hotel caters particularly well for the business traveller, and there are three conference rooms suitable for private dinners as well as for meetings. These rooms, like all the public areas in the hotel, are fully air-conditioned and have fax and telephone links.

The Phoenix Hotel

1-8 Kensington Gardens Square London W2 4BH
Tel 071 229 2494 Fax 071 727 1419 Telex 298854 PHENIX

130 rooms with bath or shower, telephone, tv, radio, mini bars in some suites, teasmade on request, hairdryer, iron on request • snacks from room service from 7 a.m. to 11 p.m, English and Continental breakfast, laundry and dry cleaning • business services, safe, no conference room • in-house brasserie: Café Phoenix • lift, meter parking • no animals • single room ££, double room £, Continental breakfast included, all major credit cards • tube: Bayswater; bus nos: 15, 36, 70

Situated in Bayswater, the Phoenix Hotel opened in 1960. It is a listed building dating from 1854, overlooking an attractive garden square. The surrounding area used to be called Tyburnia, from the famous Tyburn gallows at Marble Arch.

Recently immaculately restored by its private owners, this is one of the more reasonably priced London hotels. In the large open foyer we were welcomed by friendly staff and taken by lift to view a selection of the 130 rooms.

The hotel has a number of spacious split-level family rooms. All the bedrooms have pickled pine furniture, a writing desk, good-sized mirrors and pretty arrangements of dried flowers. The walls are hung with prints and the brass lamps

• • • • • • • • • •

are green-shaded to give a cosy atmosphere. The bathrooms are well designed with refreshing pink and grey tiles, strong efficient showers and a generous array of toiletries.

On the ground floor is a lounge bar where cricketing fans will be delighted to find a collection of prints featuring famous players and famous matches. The bar is wood-panelled, with comfortable high stools, elegant tub chairs and swagged pelmetted curtains in blue, grey and peach. Behind the lounge is the Snug. Here a coal fire burns and portraits in oils look down from the wood-panelled walls.

In the dining area, used for breakfast only, plenty of plants refreshingly contrast with a wooden floor, grey and pink marble-topped tables, heavy tapestry curtains and modern pictures.

Royal Cambridge Hotel

124 Sussex Gardens London W2 1UB
Tel 071 873 0000 Fax 071 873 0830

30 rooms, 16 with bath, 14 with shower, telephone, satellite tv, radio, hairdryer, trouserpress (no mini bar or teasmade) • room service with snacks, English and Continental breakfast, laundry, dry cleaning • business services, safe (no conference room) • nearest restaurant: San Martino • lift, parking for 8 cars • no animals • single room £, double room £, including full English breakfast, all major credit cards • tube: Paddington; bus nos: 7, 15, 36

This Victorian hotel is part of a charming terrace – Cambridge Terrace – and was originally two townhouses. It is privately owned and has been in the same family for over 13 years. In 1991 the hotel underwent extensive refurbishment and now provides very welcoming and attractive accommodation for both tourists and business travellers.

• • • • • • • • •

There is definitely a new trend in London towards small, intimate, well run and reasonably priced establishments where guests are not just a room number but greeted by name and looked after with every consideration, and The Royal Cambridge is one such. We were warmly received on our arrival and felt at home straight away.

The reception area is decorated in soft shades of pink and lilac, and a brass chandelier illuminates arrangements of fragrant flowers. A small lounge off the reception – a convenient place to wait for friends – has comfy sofas in blue and purple. The lilac walls are hung with prints and huge pot plants give an airy feel.

The bedrooms are decorated in a modern classical style, some with dark wooden wardrobes and matching dressing tables, and others with chairs, wardrobes, dressing tables and headboards all in pickled pine. In some rooms draped canopies above the beds echoed the curtains at the window, and the colours were mainly delicate pastels. No two rooms seemed completely alike. The bathrooms are tiled in pale pink and the tile design incorporates an unusual bathing beauty motif. The showers are strong and plenty of toiletries are provided.

All the rooms had the facilities the modern traveller has come to expect, such as satellite television, direct-dial telephone and a trouserpress. Many guests will appreciate the telephone extension in the bathroom and the extra powerpoint provided for plugging in a personal computer or fax. We thought the facilities very good at such a reasonable price.

A full English breakfast is included in the tariff and can be taken downstairs in the pretty dining room. The breakfast menu offers plenty of choice, including eggs and bacon, porridge and cornflakes. For anyone returning exhausted in the evening there is a bar behind the reception area that will serve anything from fruit juice to a glass of champagne.

Whites Hotel

Lancaster Gate London W2 3NR
Tel 071 262 2711 Fax 071 262 2147 Telex 24771

54 air-conditioned rooms with bath, telephone, satellite and movie channel tv, radio, mini bar, teasmade on request, hairdryer, trouserpress on request, safe • 24-hour room service, hot and cold snacks, English and Continental breakfast, laundry, dry cleaning, valet service • business services, 2 conference rooms • in-house restaurant • lift, parking on forecourt • no animals • single room £££, double room £££, suite ££££, excluding breakfast, all major credit cards • tube: Lancaster Gate; bus nos: 12, 94

This beautiful white Victorian mansion overlooking Hyde Park is entrancing at night: the façade is cleverly floodlit and the trees twinkle with white fairy lights. We drove into the cobbled forecourt and our car was parked for us as we were welcomed through tunnelled glass canopies into this hotel of character and distinction.

In the eighteenth century there was a herb and tea garden owned by Sir John Hill on the site of Whites Hotel. A terrace of superior private residences was built there in 1866, and its architect Sancton Wood, had he lived another ten years,

• • • • • • • • • •

would have been gratified to discover it hailed in *The Building News* as "the most handsome terrace in London or any city in the world".

Numbers 90-92 Lancaster Gate became a hotel in 1924, and have been operating as Whites Hotel since 1949. In 1987 a three-year refurbishment was completed, and now this establishment represents the epitome of traditional English style and gracious formal living.

Management in tailcoats greeted us in the magnificent reception area, which featured an ornate gilded mirror over a working fire, a fine carpet, crystal chandeliers, Chinese porcelain, and a splendid yew reception desk. An inspection of the public rooms discovered the quiet Writing Room, wood-panelled and elegantly furnished with a resplendent stained-glass dome inset into the ceiling.

The bar, complete with sunny terrace overlooking Royal Kensington Gardens, has a large and interesting collection of caricature engravings, carved figures and porcelain, displayed against primrose-coloured walls. The Grill Room is classically elegant in peach and cream, its ornate ceiling hung with chandeliers. The restaurant, with its white marble and palm trees, offers a traditional menu of old favourites, such as melon with ginger or prawn salad, followed by rainbow trout, chicken breast in mushroom sauce, veal or steak, with a trifle or fruit salad to round off the meal.

In our bedroom we found the height of luxury. Swagged silk moiré drapes swept to the floor, and the muted colour scheme was softly lit by crystal wall lights. The television set was cleverly concealed and emerged from its hiding place at the press of a button.

The marble bathrooms have been imported from Italy, complete with gilded glass shower screens and brass fittings, and are generously equipped with toiletries.

• • • • • • • • • •

Westminster Belgravia

Westminster and Belgravia occupy a stretch of land south of St James's Park and Buckingham Palace in the curve of the Thames below Westminster Bridge.

Westminster, as even those who have never visited London before probably know, is a district largely given over to government offices; comparatively few people reside here. Just north of Westminster Bridge is Whitehall, home of the Admiralty, the Old War Office, the Foreign Office and the Treasury. Just off Whitehall, near the Cenotaph, which commemorates the fallen in both World Wars, is Downing Street. The Prime Minister's residence is at Number Ten, and the Chancellor lives next door at Number Eleven.

Just south of Westminster Bridge are the Houses of Parliament in the Palace of Westminster. This stunning Victorian medieval building with its clock tower, Big Ben, has come to represent democracy throughout the world. It is thought that a royal palace was first built on this site in about 1000, next to an existing monastery, which has become Westminster Abbey. Councils of noblemen, the forerunner of the House of Lords, met here from around 1098. In 1265 Simon de Montfort instituted the practice of calling a further council made up of knights and burghers who represented the shires and towns. This was the forerunner of the House of Commons.

From this time on, the monarch strove to control the representatives, who were initially sent to advise him, but they gradually got the upper hand because the monarch needed their taxes. During the eighteenth century, parliament gained supremacy, and government by parliament became an irrefutable reality.

Visitors may listen to debates in the Commons and the Lords, but to be sure of a seat should apply to either an MP or Peer, or to the Commons Public Information Office, well in advance.

Far left: Part of the Queen Victoria Memorial in front of Buckingham Palace.

Left: Ceremonial at Buckingham Palace never fails to draw a crowd.

Westminster Abbey, across St Margaret Street from the Houses of Parliament, is Britain's mother church. While still unfinished, it was chosen on Christmas Day 1066 by William the Conqueror for his coronation, and ever since it has been the scene of the coronations, marriages and burials of British monarchs. It is a fine gothic building and the burial place of poets and national heroes.

Westminster Cathedral is London's most important and most imposing Roman Catholic church, and a building of great originality, a Byzantine basilica constructed between 1895 and 1903 on the model of Santa Sophia in Istanbul.

In Belgravia, an exclusive residential district just south of Buckingham Palace, are to be found some of London's most handsome terraces. These were built by Thomas Cubitt and another distinguished architect, Basevi, for the aristocracy shortly after Buckingham Palace was established as the monarch's seat in the 1820s. Belgrave Square, Eaton Square and Chester Square are classically appealing, and today the home of some of the nation's wealthiest people.

Victoria Station, serving the southeast and affording a link to the Continent via Dover, is located in the west of Belgravia, and travellers intending to explore other parts of Britain may also make use of the Victoria Coach Station, which is situated between Semley Place and Elizabeth Street.

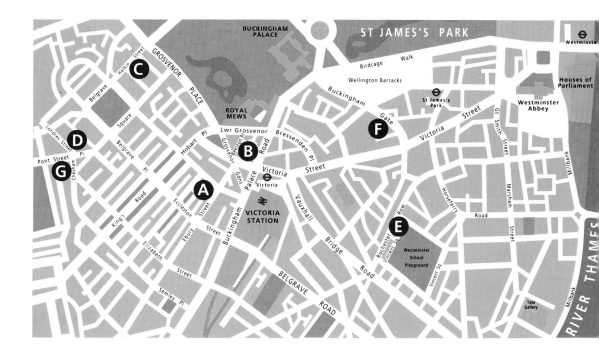

A Ebury Court Hotel

B The Goring Hotel

C The Halkin

D The Lowndes: A Hyatt Hotel

E The Rochester Hotel

F St James's Court

G Sheraton Belgravia

⊖ London Underground

⇌ British Rail

*Left: Big Ben, with Boadicea's statue
in the foreground.*

Ebury Court Hotel

28 Ebury Street London SW1W OLU
Tel 071 730 8147 Fax 071 823 5966

46 rooms (some four-posters), 26 with bath, 2 with shower, 18 without
facilities; telephone, satellite tv, radio, teasmade, hairdryer,
trouserpress on request, no air conditioning • 24-hour room service,
hot and cold snacks (no mini bar), English and Continental breakfast,
laundry, dry cleaning • business services, safe, conference rooms for up to
30 people • in-house restaurant: Tophams • lift, NCP and meter parking •
animals welcome by arrangement • single room £, double room ££–£££,
including breakfast, all major credit cards • tube: Victoria;
bus nos: C1, 2B, 11, 16, 24, 25, 29, 36, 38, 52, 73, 135

This hotel is within a stone's throw of Victoria Station. The pretty façade is
decorated with a profusion of plants and flowers in window boxes and tumbling
over the railings.

• • • • • • • • • •

The Ebury Court Hotel offers a wide range of rooms at competitive prices that include a full English or Continental breakfast. The rooms without facilities are equipped with towelling robes and the separate bathrooms are only a few steps along the corridor. All the other rooms have attractive en suite bathrooms with well lit mirrors, and the bedrooms are simply and elegantly furnished, with lovely chests of drawers, antique mirrors, chintz curtains, and some four-posters. There is one triple room.

In addition to the main building, the hotel owns an adjacent mews house used for longer rentals. The Ebury Court Hotel was founded by Diana Topham and her brother over 50 years ago and is still owned and run by the same family.

There is a sitting room with comfortable sofas, a cosy alcoved breakfast room downstairs, and upstairs a new restaurant called Topham's, which serves lunch and dinner. The menu is small, but changes regularly and features established favourites, such as Dover sole, fillet steak and Scotch salmon amongst its traditional dishes. The paintings on the walls are by the great-great-great grandfather of the present owner. Lace curtains and charmingly shaded candles give an intimate Edwardian feel to this pretty room.

Another feature of this hotel is its private drinking club, which is open to residents. The club room gives on to a garden room that doubles as an art gallery, and itself leads out to an eye-catching patio garden. For visitors from the United States there is a complimentary itinerary planning service.

The head porter is renowned for his ability to obtain even the most sought-after theatre and opera tickets and he also has a talent for racing tips. The staff are welcoming and friendly and seem to have an encyclopaedic memory for guests' names and faces.

The Goring Hotel

Beeston Place Grosvenor Gardens London SW1W 0JW
Tel 071 834 8211 Fax 071 834 4393 Telex 919166

84 rooms, many with air conditioning, all with bath and shower, telephone, satellite tv, radio, hairdryer, bathrobes on request • 24-hour room service, hot and cold snacks (no mini bar), full and light English breakfast, Continental breakfast, laundry, dry cleaning and full valet service • business services, 5 conference rooms, safe • in-house restaurant serves traditional English and European cuisine • lift, limited parking • no animals • single room £££, double room £££, suite £££, excluding breakfast, all major credit cards • tube: Victoria; bus nos: C1, 11, 25, 36, 38

O. R. Goring opened his establishment in March 1910, announcing that it was the first hotel in the world with a private bathroom and central heating to every bedroom. His motto was: "When your name is above the door, you try that much harder!" Today the hotel is run by the third generation of Gorings; their motto remains proudly the same.

The Edwardian building is in the Adam style with a classic portico, and

• • • • • • • • •

impeccably kept and decorated with colourful flowering window boxes. It is situated within hailing distance of Buckingham Palace and the famous Queen's Gallery.

The friendly doorman welcomed us into a gracious apricot and cream entrance hall with classic double arches and a black and white marble floor. The spacious Garden Lounge, where guests can relax over a pot of coffee or indulge in warm scones and fresh cream with a traditional afternoon tea, continues the mellow colour scheme. There are elegant chairs and brown leather button-backed chesterfields. A life-sized woolly sheep sits in front of an open fire; other members of its family are to be found in some of the bedrooms.

The bar enjoys a good view of the garden, which is unfortunately not open to residents. At the other end of the lobby is the Goring Restaurant. Traditional in style, the dining room has a magnificent pale green ceiling embellished with plasterwork. English and European dishes prevail, with seasonal game one of the specialities. The chef offers traditional British cuisine with a modern influence, and the superb selection of wines on the extensive list made us wish that we had

more time to sample them.

The bedrooms are very individual in colour scheme and furnishing, spacious, light and well appointed. We appreciated the roomy storage space. Our bathroom was palatial, finished in black and cream Italian marble, with plenty of shelf space and deluxe double washbasins. Some of the suites have superb tiled balconies with a pretty wrought-iron table for four overlooking the lawn and mature shrubberies below.

Service at The Goring has a personal quality that reflects the family's continued dedication to its clients, some of whom are the grandchildren of the hotel's original guests.

The Halkin

Halkin Street London SW1X 7DJ
Tel 071 333 1000 Fax 071 333 1100 Telex 290308 HALKIN

41 luxury air-conditioned rooms with bath and shower, telephone, fax, safe, tv (Sky), video, video library, bathrobes and slippers, natural sponges, toiletries, hairdryer, mini bar • 24-hour room service with hot and cold snacks, English and Continental breakfast, laundry, dry cleaning • full business services including Reuters room, conference room • in-house restaurant with French and Italian cuisine • lift, car valet service, NCP parking • no animals except guide dogs • single room ££££, double room ££££, suite ££££, breakfast not included, all major credit cards • tube: Hyde Park Corner; bus nos: 10, 14, 19, 22, 36, 74, 137

This spectacular hotel offers some of the finest hospitality that money can buy. Opened in the spring of 1991, The Halkin is a completely new building, though you would not know it, as its façade has been created to perfectly match the decorous architectural style of its nineteenth-century neighbours in Halkin Street at the heart of Belgravia.

Inside we were met by a startling contrast: a stunningly successful mix of ultra-modern Italian architectural design and oriental minimalism complemented by state-of-the-art technology. Throughout the hotel bold, clean lines, absolute

• • • • • • • • • •

simplicity and materials of the highest quality create a mood of understated elegance that is easy to live with. The Halkin will delight the guest who craves dramatic style and originality.

The light airy lobby has marble flooring incorporating Michelangelo's twelve-pointed star from the Piazza del Campidoglio in Rome. The harmonious colour schemes throughout the hotel symbolize the elements. The first floor is green and blue for water, the second beige and sand for air, the third pink and rust for fire, the fourth grey and black for earth, and the fifth floor, in black with a copper-domed ceiling, represents the night sky and the universe.

In the lounge are bright blue leather tub chairs, pale fawn sofas, and occasional weeping Benjamina trees. Casual drapes of white cotton are looped at the tall windows and a single white freesia in a plain glass flute creates a sensational impact, a refreshing change from the massed floral displays found in more conventional hotels.

An abstract mural enlivens the small atrium from which lifts ascend to the bedrooms. The curved corridor walls appeared to us like a finely pleated skirt: they are faced with narrow strips of black wood. The doors are flush with the walls, invisible but for a discreet number and a small red do-not-disturb light.

The bedrooms, studios and conservatory suites are architecturally dramatic. Furnishings include closets concealed in chequered rosewood-panelled walls, pale cream wild silk bedspreads and headboards, television sets that glide on swivelling arms, and electronic touch panels that control television, lights, air-conditioning and do-not-disturb signs, and also summon the valet and room service.

The bathrooms are impressive and superbly equipped. There are nice touches like anti-mist mirrors, natural sponges and a stock of Penhaligon toiletries. In the rooms guests are provided with bathrobes and slippers, an umbrella, a shopping bag and a clothes brush.

We were disappointed not to find a bar, but were reassured that one would soon be incorporated. However, we were consoled by the lovely food in the restaurant

overlooking the garden. The atmosphere is enchanting and the menu inspired.

The Halkin's staff must be the best dressed in London: their uniforms were designed by Georgio Armani. The hotel operates a unique policy with regard to their staff: no tipping.

The Lowndes: A Hyatt Hotel

21 Lowndes Street London SW1X 9ES
Tel 071 235 6020 Fax 071 235 1154 Telex 919066

**78 air-conditioned rooms with bath and shower, telephone, satellite tv
with CNN and Sky, radio, mini bar, trouserpress, hairdryer, bathrobes,
safe; scales in suites • room service with hot and cold snacks from 6 a.m.
to midnight, English and Continental breakfast, laundry,
dry cleaning • business services, conference room • in-house
restaurant: The Lowndes Brasserie • lift, NCP and meter parking •
no animals except guide dogs • single room ££££, double room ££££,
suite ££££, breakfast not included, all major credit cards and JCB •
tube: Knightsbridge; bus nos: C1, 19, 22, 137**

This hotel is situated in the heart of Belgravia within easy walking distance of
Harrods and the exclusive boutiques of Sloane Street. Complete refurbishment
in 1991 has brought to the hotel the relaxed and elegant style of an English
country house.

• • • • • • • • • •

To one side of the marbled foyer is the lobby lounge, and the centrepiece of this area is a lovely fireplace with a leather club fender. One wall is panelled in limed oak, with shelves full of books and alcoves with trompe l'oeil paintings. Easy chairs and comfortable sofas covered in eye-catching checks are placed round low coffee tables, and here we had tea, which came in a stylish chrome flask on a tray with Wedgwood china and fresh roses.

The Lowndes Brasserie, just off the lobby, has a bar finished in black granite. The walls are pine-panelled and hung with Raoul Dufy prints. The large windows open on to the terrace at the front, and an abundance of dried flowers in copper, pewter and earthenware pots decorate the window sills. The chairs are in tartan or stripes, and the menu comes on a wooden board. The food is very reasonably priced, and the selection includes a three-course lunch served on a wooden suchi board.

At the back of the ground floor is the Library, the hotel's elegant meeting room with burr elm panelling and ice-blue wallpaper. A large burr elm table seats up to 14 people, and a bookcase houses an up-to-date audio-visual system.

The first and second floors are no-smoking areas. All 78 rooms are double glazed with individually controlled air conditioning. The décor is pleasant and inviting and similar in all rooms, except in the suites; eight rooms have balconies overlooking the courtyard.

The rooms have stunning interior-lit wardrobes housing a trouserpress and safe, and a writing desk with make-up mirror. The mini bar is replenished with ice and nuts each evening and fresh plants change according to the season. The bathrooms are finished in marble with power showers and natural toiletries from Taylors of London. Regular guests are provided with monogrammed bathrobes for their personal use.

We stayed in the Biedermeier Suite. Here we found built-in bookshelves full of antiquarian books, a marble fireplace, a dining table for six and huge deep sofas. We had a beautifully canopied bed and a large bathroom with a heated towel rail and a bidet.

Another feature of a particularly enjoyable stay was access to The Peak, a fully equipped fitness centre nearby, owned by a sister hotel, The Hyatt Carlton. Charges may be billed directly to your room.

The Rochester Hotel

69 Vincent Square London SW1 2PA
Tel 071 828 6611 Fax 071 233 6724 Telex 8813164

67 rooms with bath and shower, telephone, satellite tv, radio, hairdryer, trouserpress (no mini bar or teasmade) • 24-hour room service, hot and cold snacks, English and Continental breakfast, laundry, dry cleaning • business services, safe, 3 conference rooms, air conditioning in public areas • in-house restaurant: The Pavilion, and Vincent's Wine Bar • lift, meter parking • animals welcome by arrangement • single room £££, double room £££, suite ££, breakfast not included, all major credit cards • tube: Victoria; bus nos: C1, 2B, 11, 16, 24, 25, 29, 36, 38, 52, 73, 135

This handsome mid-Victorian building is situated close to Victoria Station on the corner of Rochester Row and Vane Street. It overlooks the cricket pitch in Vincent Square: we were surprised to find such a quiet location so close to the heart of town.

The hotel has undergone recent extensive renovation and meets the high standards the modern traveller has come to expect. The sumptuous foyer with its marble floor has a wealth of green plants and a central lift made entirely of glass and polished brass.

The rooms and suites are spacious and some have a private balcony. Predominating colours are soft blues, pinks, greens and golds. The rosewood furniture was handmade in China. We were particularly impressed by the Syndicate Rooms, in which the beds slide flush into the walls so that the rooms can be transformed for meetings. All the bathrooms are finished in marble and there are luxurious bathrobes and a good supply of toiletries.

Lords Lounge Bar with its stylish rosewood décor is a relaxing and comfortable place for a pre-dinner drink. It leads on to The Pavilion Restaurant, where we sampled a light lunch from an exciting menu. We liked the light airy feel of the dining room, which has a stained glass window set into the ceiling, and tables laid with pink linen.

Vincent's Wine Bar, the hotel's other eating place, has its own entrance from the street, and many non-residents drink here and choose from the interesting Mediterranean menu. The wine bar has a lively informal atmosphere.

The business traveller is well catered for at The Rochester, with conference and banqueting suites offering facilities for management meetings, exhibitions, seminars, and audio-visual presentations. Private dinner parties can also be arranged.

• • • • • • • • • •

St James's Court

Buckingham Gate London SW1E 6AF
Tel 071 834 6655 Fax 071 630 7587 Telex 930875 TAJJAM G

400 rooms and 80 apartments with bath and shower, including a block of
27 luxury suites, telephone, cable tv, radio, mini bar (no teasmade)
hairdryer, bathrobes • health club, 24-hour room service, hot and cold
snacks, English and Continental breakfast, laundry, dry cleaning • business
centre, conference rooms, offices, safe, air conditioning • 3 in-house
restaurants: Chinese, French, international • lifts, NCP parking •
no animals • single room ££££, double room ££££, suite £££–££££,
breakfast not included, all major credit cards • tube: Victoria;
bus nos: C1 2B 11, 16, 24, 25, 29, 36, 38, 52

This splendid Edwardian building in the City of Westminster was commissioned in
1896 by the Crown to house the overflow of visitors to Buckingham Palace. It first
opened in 1903 and comprises eight interconnecting buildings with arched windows
and balconies surrounding a central courtyard. Its magnificent terracotta frieze is

• • • • • • • • • •

the longest continual frieze in the world and depicts scenes from Shakespeare's plays. The courtyard was redesigned by Lord Kenilworth in 1985 and now colourful gardens and paved walkways of York stone are laid out round the fountain said to have been donated by Queen Victoria.

The hotel combines comfort with traditional style in its 400 bedrooms, including 19 suites, and 80 fully serviced self-contained apartments.

The main foyer is luxuriously finished in warm mahogany and classic cool marble and the leather Chesterfields give this palatial room a masculine feel. The bedrooms are individually designed to one of eight colour schemes. Our room was enormous and high-ceilinged, with carved headboards on the beds, deep blue and peach bedspreads, and curtains to match. We particularly appreciated the fresh flowers and the deep comfortable chairs. The bathroom was very large and uncluttered, and well equipped with Molton Brown toiletries.

The apartments are reached via the courtyard and range from spacious studios to stately three-bedroomed complexes. Each apartment has its own fully equipped kitchen and a stunningly designed living room of grand proportions to allow guests to entertain in style. The Presidential Suite occupies an astounding 13 rooms! This wing of St James's Court, an all-suite block known as Falconers, has its own manager and staff, though of course all the hotel facilities are open to residents.

For the business traveller there is the Chambers Business Centre with five offices, two lounge receptions, three boardrooms, three committee rooms and full multilingual secretarial services. The hotel also offers four salons equipped for banqueting and receptions for up to 300 people.

Fitness enthusiasts and the health-conscious will be delighted with the facilities at the Olympian Health Club. Here we found two gymnasiums, a sunbed, two whirlpools, two saunas, two steamrooms, two massage rooms and staff who will arrange a personal fitness programme for any guest who asks for it.

St James's Court has three restaurants. The Inn of Happiness was the first restaurant to introduce the Chinese buffet lunch to London; the informal Café Mediterranée offers light meals and refreshments; and the Auberge de Provence, under the same management as the famous l'Ousteau de Baumanière in France, is one of London's premier French restaurants.

Sheraton Belgravia

20 Chesham Place London SW1X 8HQ
Tel 071 235 6040 Fax 071 259 6243 Telex 919020

89 air-conditioned rooms with bath and shower, telephone, satellite tv, radio, mini bar, hairdryer, bathrobes • full 24-hour room service, English and Continental breakfast, laundry, dry cleaning • business services, 2 conference rooms, safe • in-house restaurant: Chesham's • lift, meter parking, valet • animals welcome by arrangement • single room ££££, double room ££££, breakfast not included, all major credit cards, including En Route, JCB, Carte Blanche • tube: Knightsbridge; bus nos: C1, 19, 22, 137

The Sheraton Belgravia reopened in February 1991 after complete refurbishment to all its public areas. We found this imposing modern building in one of Belgravia's leafy squares: unusually for a Sheraton it has only 89 rooms, all of which are individually furnished in the traditional English townhouse style.

The magnificent foyer and lounge are panelled in bird's eye maple. Comfy sofas are arranged in quiet alcoves and an intimate and informal atmosphere is achieved through the use of warm relaxing colours: green, sand, burgundy and gold. Soft

• • • • • • • • • •

furnishings are plain or striped rather than floral.

The staff welcomed us with a complimentary glass of champagne, which we sipped while we were being checked in – a delightful gesture that readied us for a pleasant stay. Our bedroom had elegant Regency furniture. The beds were extra large, and the colour scheme was yellow and grey, with checked curtains and matching bedspread. We sat by the window with the sun streaming in and enjoyed a cool drink. There are fresh flowers in every room and air-conditioning ensures a good night's sleep even in the hottest weather. In the bathroom we found enormous towels, bathrobes and a telephone extension.

The hotel offers 24-hour room service, but we decided to try the in-house restaurant, Chesham's. This restaurant has its own distinctive style. There are intimate seating areas with just one table, perfect for a discreet tête-à-tête, and there is also a striking circular room with a large palm tree beneath a central glass dome. Here we found large mirrors and stone-coloured walls, and an atmosphere of Continental sophistication. The menu is an inventive mix of French and English cuisine. At lunch time guests can choose a set menu with unlimited house wine. Afternoon tea with Devonshire cream scones and homemade jam can be enjoyed in deep leather chairs in the wood-panelled bar or in the hotel lounge.

Knightsbridge Chelsea

T his area extends from the south side of Hyde Park down to the Thames at Cheyne Walk and the Chelsea Embankment. Hyde Park is the largest open space in London. Here the visitor can go boating on the Serpentine, the lake made in 1730, or ride a horse along Rotten Row. In the centre of the park is a bird sanctuary, and near this is Jacob Epstein's statue "Rima". In the northeast corner of Hyde Park is Speaker's Corner. This was established in 1872 as a place where orators drew crowds to listen to their eccentric views, but it has recently gained a more serious reputation thanks to speakers coming from countries where freedom of speech is denied. Sunday is the best day for listening. Hyde Park Corner, in the southeast, is the gateway to Knightsbridge, an area of dignified residences and home to some of London's finest museums.

The museums are served by a tunnel leading directly to them from South Kensington tube station. The complex of museums incorporating the Science Museum, the Natural History Museum and the Victoria & Albert Museum was conceived by Queen Victoria's consort Prince Albert. The Science Museum houses such attractions as machinery showing the development of steam power and full-scale models of modern space and underwater craft. On permanent exhibition is Stephenson's "Rocket", the

• • • • • • • • •

famous pioneer locomotive, and equally popular are the Launch Pad, where visitors can work the machines themselves, and Food for Thought, which shows how we buy, prepare and eat food.

The Natural History Museum houses a wonderful collection of huge dinosaur skeletons, as well as a Discovery Centre where children can do their own exploring, a permanent exhibition called Discovering Mammals, and another of gemstones. The Victoria & Albert is probably the world's greatest museum of the decorative arts, with fabulous collections of historical costumes, furniture, household implements, pottery and art.

Knightsbridge is of course also famous for Harrods, London's biggest and best department store, and in general this area is a paradise for the well-heeled and discerning shopper. Chelsea, Sloane Street and the King's Road are the places to shop for women's clothes. Sloane Street has top-price chic from boutiques such as Joseph Bis, Joseph Tricot, Esprit, Kenzo, Krizia, Valentino, Giorgio Armani and Katharine Hamnett. Just off Sloane Street through Pont Street is Beauchamp Place, and here you will find Bruce Oldfield, The Beauchamp Place Shop, Monsoon, and Caroline Charles.

The King's Road offers a complete contrast. This is where punk originated, and it is the home of Vivienne Westwood's designs, centred on World's End and Boys. The thoroughfare is famous for its bizarre if

ephemeral fashions, which can be seen not only in the shops, but also modelled by the people who parade there. The liveliest time to visit is a Saturday afternoon.

Far left: Harrods, arguably the most famous monument in the Brompton Road.

Left: Done to a turn! A Chelsea pensioner demonstrates his skill with a frying pan.

The King's Road runs through what is otherwise a quiet and elegant village; only in the late eighteenth century did Chelsea become part of London. In 1682 Charles II built the Royal Hospital here as a refuge for disabled soldiers. Today it houses around 400 Chelsea Pensioners, who can be recognized by their very smart military uniforms, red in summer and blue in winter. In May each year the Royal Hospital is the venue for the Chelsea Flower Show, the greatest of Britain's horticultural events.

Another connection with horticulture is the Chelsea Physic Garden, established in 1673 by the Society of Apothecaries. Here exotic trees and shrubs, aromatic plants and herbs are cultivated for the study of medicine. The Garden is open daily during the Chelsea Flower Show, and during the summer months on Wednesday and Sunday afternoons.

Above: The Albert Bridge connects Chelsea to Battersea.

Right: Chelsea chic.

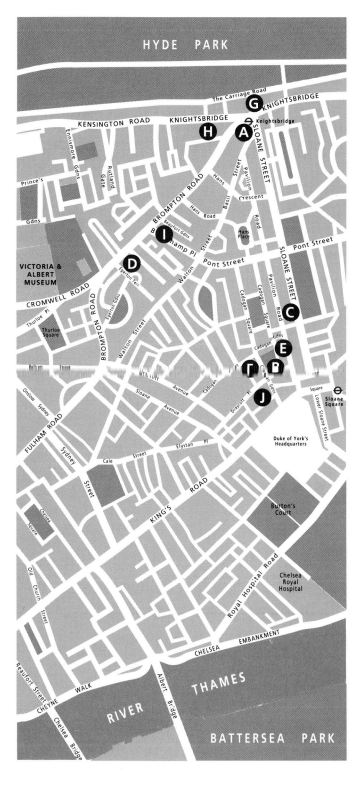

A The Basil Street Hotel

B The Draycott

C Durley House

D The Egerton House Hotel

E Eleven Cadogan Gardens

F The Fenja

G Hyde Park Hotel

H Knightsbridge Green Hotel

I The Parkes Hotel

J The Sloane Hotel

⊖ London Underground

The Basil Street Hotel

Knightsbridge, London SW3 1AH
Tel 071 581 3311   Fax 071 581 3693   Telex 28379

93 rooms, 81 with bath and shower, 12 without facilities, telephone, tv, radio, hairdryer • 24-hour room service, hot and cold snacks, English and Continental breakfast, laundry, dry cleaning • business services, safe, 4 conference rooms • in-house restaurant with English cuisine, also coffee shop, wine bar, sandwich bar, Parrot Club • lift, NCP and meter parking • one dog per room allowed by arrangement • single room £–£££, double room £–£££, suite £££, breakfast not included; all major credit cards • tube: Knightsbridge; bus nos: C1 10, 19, 22, 52, 74, 137

In the heart of Knightsbridge, our favourite shopping area, 191 steps away from Harrods, 89 steps from Harvey Nichols, is this eccentric hotel. It was built on the site of an old Underground station in 1910, and extended in 1936 when a magnificent reception lounge took the place of the old booking hall. Today this area has been transformed into the Parrot Club, an exclusive club for women. It is so called because a parrot called Basil used to live in the hotel.

The Parrot Club is essentially a club for women only. Those who are not resident in the hotel have to pay an annual membership fee, but for residents the club is free. Members have their parcels delivered to the Club, relax after shopping with a glass of champagne, and invite guests to join them at the bar. Men are

allowed in by invitation only. There is a luxurious powder room, equipped with everything including heated rollers, and a baby minding service.

All the public areas of this hotel are filled with antique furniture, oriental carpets, oil paintings and elegant mirrors. We walked from the hall up a Georgian staircase to a large lounge. There we sat in comfortable chintz chairs and rang the bell to summon a waiter to bring our afternoon tea.

Our favourite public room was the Long Gallery, which has windowed alcoves on one side, each one with its own writing desk. This is the perfect place for writing a *billet doux* before continuing along the corridor with its antique vases and wood- blocked floor to the dining room. This is a grand old-fashioned room with walls of pale green. Luncheon is a

relaxed affair with a fixed menu of either two or three courses. Dinner is by candlelight and at the piano a student from the Royal College of Music recreates a mood of bygone days. For more simple meals, guests can choose the coffee shop or the wine bar in the cellar.

The bedrooms are large and sumptuously furnished. Many of the bathrooms are very generously proportioned; some are pine-panelled, others tiled. The rooms without private facilities are one of the best bargains in town, as their bathrooms are right next door.

• • • • • • • • • •

The Draycott

24-26 Cadogan Gardens London SW3 2RP
Tel 071 730 6466 Fax 071 730 0236 Telex 914947 DRAYCT G

25 rooms with bath and shower, telephone, satellite and cable tv, CNN, video on request, radio, hairdryer, bathrobes, mini bar • 24-hour room service, English and Continental breakfast, laundry, dry cleaning • business services, safe, no conference room • nearest restaurants: Ma Cuisine, Waltons, Bibendum • lift, meter parking • no animals • single room ££–£££, double room £££–££££, suite £££, excluding breakfast, all major credit cards • tube: Sloane Square; bus nos: 137, C1, 11, 19, 22

Tucked behind fashionable King's Road around the corner from Sloane Square is The Draycott, haunt of international celebrities and voted "most romantic city hotel" by America's *Travel and Leisure* magazine. The Draycott gives a feeling of privacy and seclusion: the reception desk is small and discreet, and guests are

• • • • • • • • • •

welcomed into the smoking room, where they can be served from the bar and, in the winter, enjoy the warmth of the open fire.

The drawing room, with its antique furniture, fine china and paintings, is elegant and formal in soft pink and green. Snacks can be served here and in fine weather guests may wander out through the french windows into the hotel's beautiful private garden to take afternoon tea.

The building comprises two townhouses joined together, and the bedrooms are served by two staircases and a lift. The Draycott's 25 bedrooms are all individually decorated and offer ample wardrobe space.

At the top of the price range the lavish four-poster suite is very large and light, with a deeply comfortable bed and sofa. Interior designer Julie Hodges has restored the house's original features where possible, and some of the rooms have working fireplaces and balconies overlooking the garden. All the rooms are equipped with refrigerated bars and satellite colour television, and stunning arrangements of fresh flowers. The bathrooms have good strong showers.

The Draycott does not have a restaurant, but there is an excellent room service menu, and guests can always help themselves from the antique stone vase full of

apples in the hall downstairs. The staff are unobtrusive as well as efficient. Guests have complimentary use of a health club two minutes' walk away.

Durley House

115 Sloane Street London SW1X 9PJ
Tel 071 235 5537 Fax 071 259 6977 Telex 919235 DURLEY G

11 rooms with bath and shower, air conditioning on request, telephone, tv, radio, mini bar, kitchen, hairdryer, trouserpress, bathrobes, shoe cleaning • 24-hour room service, English and Continental breakfast, laundry, dry cleaning • business facilities, conference rooms, safe • nearest restaurant: Sale e Pepe • lift, NCP parking • suite £££-££££, breakfast not included, all major credit cards except Diners • tube: Sloane Square; bus nos: C1 11, 19, 22, 137

No hotel could be more splendidly private than Durley House. Behind its discreet façade we found an extravagant masterpiece. There is no tiresome formality in the wood-panelled reception, just a friendly receptionist behind a grand writing desk to hand over the keys.

Luckily there was only one suite available for our stay. Had there been a choice we would have found it impossible to come to a decision. Our suite was lavishly decorated and furnished, and everywhere we saw the flair of the owner's wife, an accomplished interior designer. The whole place enveloped us in such a degree of

• • • • • • • • • •

luxury that we dreaded returning to the ordinary world.

We were on the ground floor, in a room like a film set. The rose chintz curtains in the lounge overflowed in an abundance of fabric onto the carpet, and the sofa and chairs were upholstered to match. Above the carved marble fireplace hung a portrait in oils, and there were lovely prints and watercolours on the other walls. Underneath the television set we found games of Monopoly and Scrabble. On the small desk and the bureau were posies of dried flowers, and the bedroom and lounge were made homely with house plants. We enjoyed the huge American-style beds and the spacious bathroom with its fluffy towelling robes.

Each of the 11 suites has its own fully equipped kitchen, the fridge is filled with drinks, and guests are even supplied with vitamin C tablets.

The most flamboyant room must be the Piano Suite, a breathtaking piece of interior design. The large lounge has three huge french doors overlooking the private gardens across the road. Dramatic yellow checked curtains offset the incredibly ornate mantelpiece. Pride of place among the gorgeous pieces of antique furniture went to the grand piano, but most extraordinary of all was the dumb waiter. When a meal is ordered from room service, a butler arrives to set the table, and then with a clatter the food arrives direct from the kitchen. We felt like

leaving home and moving into the Piano Suite for good.

Though each suite has its own lounge, there is a small but sumptuous salon downstairs, should guests not wish to entertain in their rooms. Across the road is a tennis court for the use of local residents as well as guests from Durley House. With all the wonderful comforts it provides, we were not surprised to hear that this hotel is the favourite haunt of many showbusiness personalities.

The Egerton House Hotel

17-19 Egerton Terrace London SW3 2BX
Tel 071 589 2412 Fax 071 584 6540

28 air-conditioned rooms with bath and shower, telephone, tv with Sky and video hire, radio, mini bar, bathrobes, hairdryer • 24-hour room service, English and Continental breakfast, laundry, dry cleaning • business services, safe, conference rooms • private lunch and dinner parties arranged for 8 –16 people • lift, parking spaces • no animals or children under eight • single room ££–£££, double room ££–££££, suite ££–£££, not including breakfast, all major credit cards • tube: Knightsbridge, South Kensington; bus nos: C1, 14, 30, 74, 503

This hotel is situated a stone's throw from Harrods in one of the smartest parts of Knightsbridge. Its location is idyllic, with tree-lined squares front and back. The Egerton was opened in late 1990 after extensive restoration and refurbishment, and it offers a fine taste of English living to its guests.

The hotel's beautifully appointed bedrooms are individually decorated with fine antique furniture, innovative fabrics, prints, oil paintings and French porcelain. The

• • • • • • • • • •

drawing room, sitting room, breakfast room and study are elegantly traditional, with deep comfortable seating. The smoking room bar has deep red walls, a cream carpet and cream and soft green armchairs and sofas. Guests help themselves to drinks from a marble-topped sideboard.

Throughout the hotel, the windows are luxuriously draped and the beds generously scattered with soft cushions on bedspreads of lace or chintz. Some of the bedrooms have four-poster beds and the majority have charming views over the gardens.

Our room offered everything the international traveller has come to expect: a marbled en suite bathroom, a private bar, and satellite television. The air was fragrant with pot pourri. There is no restaurant, but room service is excellent, and breakfast consisted of a cafetière of fresh coffee, freshly squeezed orange juice, a fruit salad of fresh grapefruit, strawberries and kiwi, two perfectly boiled eggs, toast, croissants and marmalade. The whole was beautifully presented on a lace-covered tray with a complimentary newspaper and a small vase of freesias.

Standards are exceptionally high, and the service from the Savoy-trained

manager and his friendly staff is impeccable. The bill came as a pleasant surprise: The Egerton Hotel offers astounding value for money, and we look forward to visiting a sister hotel, The Franklin, due to open in June 1992.

Eleven Cadogan Gardens

11 Cadogan Gardens London SW3 2RJ
Tel 071 730 3426 Fax 071 730 5217 Telex 8813318

61 rooms with bath and shower, telephone, tv, radio on request, safe, hairdryer, bathrobes, individually controlled heating • 24-hour room service, hot and cold snacks (no mini bar), English and Continental breakfast (Continental from 6 a.m. all day), laundry, dry cleaning, garden with deckchairs and chaises longues, Range Rover, Rolls Royce • safe, business services, conference room • health club • nearest restaurants: L'Incontro, Scalini • lift, meter parking • no animals • single room ££-£££, double room ££–££££, suite £££–££££, breakfast not included, credit cards: Visa, Mastercard, Amex • tube: Sloane Square; bus nos: C1, 11, 19, 22, 137

This red-brick gabled mansion is a treasure of a hotel. From the outside you would mistake it for a private residence, for the door is closed to the general public, but ring the brass bell and you are welcomed into a panelled entrance hall fragrant with flowers and asked to sign the visitors' book. The formalities of registration and receipts for room service and drinks are banished, and this encourages the guest to feel at home.

The hotel was opened in the summer of 1949 by an eccentric Swiss gentleman

named Charles Reider for his friends and any of their acquaintances who could furnish him with a suitable letter of introduction. On one occasion a European prince arrived under a *nom de plume* and declared that he felt more at home in Number Eleven than in his palace; he stayed for a month. But if Charles Reider took a dislike to a guest, that unfortunate person was quite likely to return from a day in town to find his baggage on the doorstep and the door locked.

The oil paintings hanging on the walls of the four townhouses that comprise the hotel were discovered in the basement by the present owners when they took over from Mr Reider's executors in 1977. They complement the antiques we found in both public and private rooms. Downstairs in the panelled drawing room with its open fireplace is a green baize card table: perfect for an evening of bridge. Here you can browse through a selection of magazines and books or enjoy a Devon cream tea. Snacks may also be taken in the conservatory. Up the panelled staircase past the stained glass window are the bedrooms, individually decorated, distinctive and full of old-world charm.

The walls of our room were luxuriously fabric-covered, the chairs deeply comfortable, and there were cabinets of books and Victorian objets d'art. We enjoyed the view over the garden. On a sunny day, porters will carry deck chairs outside, so that guests can relax among the greenery.

The Garden Suite is the pride of Eleven Cadogan Gardens with its own private entrance from the street, two large double bedrooms and bathrooms, an imposing hall and a staircase that sweeps up to a long drawing room overlooking the garden. It is a favourite place for parties.

Although there is no in-house restaurant, guests can call on room service at any hour of the day or night, and there are 30 restaurants within 10 minutes' walking distance. A Rolls Royce and a Range Rover, complete with car phones, stand on call for chauffeur-driven trips. The staff are dedicated and long-serving.

The health-conscious can arrange for sessions at the hotel's own health club, Synergy, at 1 Cadogan Gardens, just up the road. Here it is possible to exercise both aerobically and anaerobically, either individually or as part of a class. There is also a fully equipped gymnasium and an ozone therapy pool with steam rooms, saunas, and massage and beauty treatment to follow.

The Fenja

69 Cadogan Gardens London SW3 2RB
Tel 071 589 7333 Fax 071 581 4958 Telex 934272 FENJA G

14 rooms, 13 with bath, one with shower; telephone, tv, radio, room bar, hairdryer, trouserpress, bathrobes, no air conditioning • room service, hot and cold snacks, English and Continental breakfast, laundry, dry cleaning • safe, business services, conference rooms • nearest restaurants: Sambuca, Oriel, The English House • lift, meter parking • no animals • single room ££, double room ££–££££, excluding breakfast, all major credit cards • tube: Sloane Square; bus nos: C1, 11, 19, 22, 137

One of London's most unusual townhouse hotels, The Fenja (pronounced "Fen-ya") was built in the 1900s in Chelsea's secluded Cadogan Gardens. After World War II a Colonel Kaulbeck purchased the house from Cadogan Estates. He so enjoyed providing hospitality to his friends that he decided to have guests around him permanently and transformed his house into a hotel. Fenja was the name of Colonel Kaulbeck's wife, and one of the conditions of sale from the Kaulbeck family was that this name should be retained.

The hotel was completely renovated and refurbished in 1986, to incorporate bathrooms in every suite, and interior designer Rupert Lord was given a brief to redecorate in the 1900s style. The suites are named after writers and artists who

lived in Chelsea at some time during their career: thus there are Turner, Sargent, Thomas Carlyle and Jane Austen rooms, to name but four.

The atmosphere in The Fenja is relaxed and elegant. Guests are encouraged to treat the establishment as their own home. Teak and green leather give the lounge a comfortable masculine feeling, and in the public rooms, as in the bedrooms, there are paintings and prints by English masters of the eighteenth and nineteenth centuries.

The bedrooms are generously proportioned and exquisitely decorated. Fireplaces, marble busts, antique bureaux and dressing tables are to be found in most rooms. The bathrooms have big stage mirrors and are supplied with soft robes and complimentary toiletries by Floris.

Additional luxuries characteristic of The Fenja are pure linen sheets and, instead of the usual mini bar, a drinks table with cut-glass tumblers and decanters offering gin, whisky and vodka. This amply makes up for the fact that there is no bar. There is no restaurant either, but limited room service is available and guests may take afternoon tea in the lounge. The Fenja's famous English breakfast is available in bed until a luxurious 2 p.m. (most hotels stop serving breakfast at 9.30 a.m). Management provides a list of recommended restaurants nearby.

At night the maid turned down our fine linen sheets, and in the morning our shoes had been cleaned and newspapers delivered to our door. The staff promise to do everything possible for their guests, "as long as it's not immoral or illegal", and reception will arrange anything from theatre tickets to a horseback ride in Rotten Row or a chauffeur-driven limousine.

Hyde Park Hotel

Knightsbridge London SW1Y 7LA
Tel 071 235 2000 Fax 071 235 4552 Telex 262057

**186 air-conditioned rooms with bath and shower, telephone, satellite
tv with 14 stations, radio, mini bar, hairdryer, bathrobes, slippers,
bathroom scales • 24-hour room service, English and Continental breakfast,
laundry, dry cleaning, valet, hairdressing • business facilities, 5 conference
rooms, safe • in-house restaurants: The Grill Room (English), The Park
Room (Italian) • lift, NCP and meter parking • no animals • single room
££££, double room ££££, suite ££££, breakfast not included,
all major credit cards, including JCB • tube: Knightsbridge;
bus nos: C1, 9, 10, 14, 19, 22, 74, 137, 503**

This grand hotel started life in 1892 as "residential chambers for gentlemen". In
1908 it reopened as the Hyde Park Hotel, and has since been home to royalty and
visiting heads of state.

Walking through the imposing entrance, we found ourselves in one of the most
beautiful marble foyers we have ever seen. The now famous marble walls were

• • • • • • • • • •

discovered under layers of wallpaper and wood panelling during refurbishment. The doorman, who has held the post for half a century, guided us to the discreet reception area. We were greeted by management in traditional pinstripes and tails, and shown to our fabulous suite on the third floor, overlooking Hyde Park.

The sitting room was elegance itself in pale blue and yellow, with opulent couches, armchairs and an ottoman. More distinction was added by two Queen Anne chairs, an antique writing bureau, Chinese lamps and vases, and a magnificent marble firelace with an ornamental mirror. The gorgeously swagged and draped curtains were in deep blue with gold fringes and the room was delicately perfumed by a pot of fresh lilies.

A butler was assigned to our suite round the clock, and he told us that Madonna had stayed there on her recent visit to London. The bedroom had a huge four-poster bed with yellow curtains, its canopy lined in blue. The walls were subtly painted in a yellow and grey blue treatment that gave a mysterious illusion of depth. There was a grey marble fireplace, more Chinese vases, potted orchids, exquisite antique furniture, and a second television.

The bathroom, like the other two rooms, was enormous. Finished in white and grey marble, it had twin washbasins, a separate toilet, a well lit make-up mirror, heated towel rails and more green plants. The private bar was housed in the entrance hall and seemed a long way from the sitting room, but with the butler in attendance that was not a problem.

All the hotel's bathrooms have natural daylight and each room has a lobby with extra wardrobe space. Televisions have 14 channels, including one devoted to hotel information.

The hotel's majestic lounge leads on to the Park Room, probably one of the most elegant dining rooms in town. A mouthwatering selection of hors d'oeuvres was laid out for lunch, and a beautiful silver boat held every imaginable kind of fruit. The menu here is sumptuously Italian. Downstairs is the oak-panelled Grill Room, where a piano player entertains guests every evening. The tables are laid with pretty baskets of fresh flowers; there is a drinks trolley, and another for smoked salmon.

The Cavalry Bar is so named because the Household Cavalry passes it every day, and this is the perfect place for an apéritif or an after-dinner liqueur.

This hotel has every service the international traveller could possibly want, including a hairdresser and a theatre booking agency.

• • • • • • • • •

Knightsbridge Green Hotel

159 Knightsbridge London SW1X 7PD
Tel 071 584 6274 Fax 071 225 1635

24 suites and rooms, each with its own bathroom, telephone, tv, radio, teasmade (no mini bar), hairdryer, trouserpress, ice bucket • soft drinks machine, coffee and cake in club room (no room service), laundry, dry cleaning, English and Continental breakfast • business services, but no safe or conference room • nearest restaurants: Signor Sassi, Montpeliano, Ménage à Trois • lift, NCP parking • no animals • single room ££, double room ££, suite £, not including breakfast, all major credit cards, not Diners • tube: Knightsbridge; bus nos: C1, 9, 10, 14, 19, 22, 52, 74, 137

This hotel is part of the island site at the junction of Knightsbridge and Knightsbridge Green, and was constructed in the late nineteenth century as purpose-built chambers. In 1966 the Marler family, the current private owners, created the

• • • • • • • • • •

Knightsbridge Green Hotel on six upper floors over the ground floor entrance at No 159. The hotel is now run by the daughter, Mrs Louis.

We soon discovered that the style of this hotel tends towards residential accommodation. English and Continental breakfast can be served only in the suites and rooms, which are extremely large and decorated to a very high standard. There is no room service, but instead a club room offers coffee, tea and cakes on the house throughout the day. An ice machine and a soft drinks vending machine are also provided.

All the rooms are refreshingly uncluttered, with hardly a frill to be seen. The suites have a comfortable sitting area with cosy armchairs and deep settees, and the alcoved windows make the rooms light and airy. There are facilities for making your own tea and coffee. In the bedrooms we found large beds and ample cupboard space. Decorative touches were the prints on the walls and pretty lamps, and we saw some original fireplaces with wooden mantelpieces.

The club room is a pleasant place to relax and there are plenty of magazines

and books to read. Sitting around the huge coffee table we enjoyed delicious cakes and chatted to fellow guests who had tips for bargain shopping.

What we liked most about this hotel was the spacious accommodation, the privacy, the reasonable prices and the unbeatable central location. Staying here is like having your own elegant apartment in the heart of town.

• • • • • • • • •

The Parkes Hotel

41-43 Beaufort Gardens London SW3 1PW
Tel 071 581 9944 Fax 071 225 3447 Telex 922488

**33 rooms, 27 with bath, all with shower, telephone, satellite tv, radio,
teasmade, hairdryer, trouserpress, iron, safe; kitchenette and mini bar
in suites • English and Continental breakfast, laundry, dry cleaning,
no room service • business services, conference room • nearest restaurants:
Montpeliano, San Lorenzo, Maroush II • lift, meter parking • no animals •
single room ££, double room £££, suite ££–£££, including
full English breakfast, all major credit cards, except Diners •
tube: Knightsbridge; bus nos: C1, 14, 30, 74, 503**

This elegant Victorian hotel is situated in a cul-de-sac off a quiet tree-lined street
in the heart of Knightsbridge, and the accommodation it provides consists mainly
of studios and suites.

• • • • • • • • •

The small, welcoming foyer is decorated in warm golden tones, and at the back is an intimate sitting room in blue and yellow, dominated by a white marble fireplace. We noticed individual touches like the brass curtain rail, prints on the walls and armfuls of fresh flowers.

All the rooms are extremely large and lavishly appointed, and some are on two levels. The suites have separate dining areas and small, well equipped kitchenettes. The fridge is full of drinks, there is a tray for tea, coffee and hot chocolate, a microwave oven, and a good range of china and cutlery. The bathrooms are prettily tiled with good strong showers, heated towel rails and plenty of toiletries.

We stayed in the one-bedroomed penthouse suite, where the colour scheme was predominantly peach. From the sitting room, with its marble fireplace, comfortable sofa and pine coffee table, it was a few steps down to the bedroom. Here we had yellow striped wallpaper and yellow floral drapes. Useful touches were a radio alarm on the bedside table and a safe concealed in the wardrobe. A large writing desk doubled as a dressing table.

Breakfast is not normally served in bed – though if you have a kitchenette, of course you may please yourself – and the light and airy breakfast room is

downstairs. A buffet breakfast is included in the hotel tariff, and is definitely worth sampling. We could choose from tea, coffee and fruit juices, different breads, cold meats and cheeses, eggs of various types, kippers, and even ravioli.

The Parkes Hotel seemed to us an ideal choice for a lengthy stay, as it offers privacy, spacious accommodation, and the chance to entertain one's guests "at home".

• • • • • • • • • •

The Sloane Hotel

29 Draycott Place London SW3 2SH
Tel 071 581 5757 Fax 071 584 1348

12 air-conditioned rooms with bath and shower, telephone, satellite tv,
video, radio and Walkman on request, bathrobes, hairdryer • 24-hour room
service, hot and cold health-conscious snacks, English, Continental and
health food breakfast, laundry, dry cleaning • business services, conference
room, safe • nearest restaurant: Le Suquet • boutique, roof terrace, nearby
health and beauty club • lift, parking • no animals • single room £, double
room ££–£££, suite ££, not including breakfast, all major credit cards •
tube: Sloane Square; bus nos: C1, 11, 19, 22, 137

In 1991 we watched this small hotel in a traditional red-brick Victorian terrace
behind the King's Road undergo a stunning transformation: the owners completely
rebuilt the interior to create 12 bedrooms and suites to their own specifications.
No expense was spared.

What we saw inside took our breath away. The reception area has an Italian
Pietra Lara stone floor, rubbed and sanded walls in earthy green, an imposing

• • • • • • • • • •

green marble fireplace and a sofa with a black wrought-iron frame.

From here we were whisked right to the top of the building to see the breakfast room, which is quite out of the ordinary. This is a south-facing lounge and roof terrace overlooking picturesque Chelsea. Outside are comfortable sun loungers and a large table set among an abundance of flowering plants. Inside, you can also relax and admire the view, or enjoy breakfast or a meal from the room service menu at one of the café tables.

Food at The Sloane is something special, with the accent on health and fresh ingredients. Nutritious juices including carrot, fresh fruit salad with yoghurt and honey, oriental chicken with a salad of organic vegetables, walnut and date bran muffins, and herbal teas were among the treats on the menu, which can also be

served in the rooms. English and Continental breakfasts are available too. Health-conscious guests may avail themselves of the facilities of a nearby health and beauty club to which The Sloane is affiliated.

The bedrooms are outstandingly imaginative, in an intriguing mix of traditional and contemporary neo-classical styles. The owners are compulsive collectors of unusual and interesting antiques, oil paintings, framed tapestries, leather-bound books and rare objets d'art. In one dazzling split-level room we found a canopied four-poster Adam bed. The fabric of the canopy matched that at the windows and even lined the glass-fronted wardrobe.

Another room was completely black and white, with fine striped wallpaper and cameos on the headboard, and a black sofa with antique scatter cushions. In other rooms there were rich papers and fabrics in jewel-like colours, intricate patterns, multi-coloured checks and contrasts of crimson and gold.

In the hotel's exclusive boutique we browsed among an exotic array of antique jewellery, decorative objets d'art, Louis Vuitton luggage, Cartier and Rolex watches, and a fine selection of perfumes by Annick Goutal, whose toiletries are featured in the en suite bathrooms.

South Kensington

Kensington, like its close neighbours, Knightsbridge and Chelsea, is a prosperous area characterized by elegant nineteenth-century terraces and villas, major shopping streets and chic backstreets full of boutiques and antique shops.

One of its most prominent buildings is Kensington Palace, home to several members of the royal family and the London residence of the Prince and Princess of Wales. William and Mary first made it a royal residence when they bought it in 1689. Though the palace is composed mainly of private quarters, the State apartments may be visited. Some of these rooms are just as Sir Christopher Wren left them after his rebuilding works in the 1720s. The Queen's Bedroom is particularly fine. The Court Dress collection was opened on the ground floor in 1984 and includes Princess Diana's wedding gown.

The palace grounds, originally private, are now Kensington Gardens, home of the enchanting statue of Peter Pan. Also in the gardens are a bandstand, the Serpentine Gallery and the Albert Memorial. This ornate tribute to Queen Victoria's husband, who encouraged the arts and sciences and conceived the idea for the museums just south of the park, is a gothic embarrassment. Not so the Albert Hall, just opposite. This simple round

• • • • • • • • • •

structure was built between 1867 and 1871. Round the top runs a ceramic frieze illustrating the triumph of the arts and sciences. The Albert Hall is used for all kinds of exhibitions, for tennis and boxing and, most famously, for the summer season of Promenade Concerts.

Next to the Albert Hall is the Royal College of Art, and to the east is the Royal Geographical Society, a house in the Dutch style designed by Norman Shaw in 1874. In Prince Consort Road is Imperial College, the leading science department of London University, and the Royal College of Music. The college's collection of musical instruments is open to the public during term time on Mondays and Wednesdays.

Linley Sambourne House, the home of the famous cartoonist, great-grandfather of Princess Margaret's former husband Lord Snowdon, and situated at 18 Stafford Terrace, is run by the Victorian Society, and open to the public during the summer on Wednesdays and Sunday afternoons. It houses a wonderful collection of Victoriana, including photographs, clocks,

Above: A view from Kensington Palace.

Left: The Royal Albert Hall, Kensington Gore, home of the Proms.

china and glass, and the walls are decorated with original William Morris paper.

No visitor to this area should neglect the Fulham Road. Here you can find Michelin House, a gem of Art Nouveau built in 1910, which now houses the Conran Shop and Bibendum restaurant. The Conran Shop is one of the leading interior design establishments in the country, along with the fabric and wallpaper shops of Osborne & Little and Tricia Guild nearby.

Left: The Albert Memorial in Hyde Park.

A Aster House Hotel

B Blakes Hotel

C The Cranley Hotel

D Five Sumner Place Hotel

E The Gore

F Hotel 167

G John Howard Hotel

H Number Sixteen Sumner Place

I The Pelham Hotel

J Sydney House Hotel

⊖ London Underground

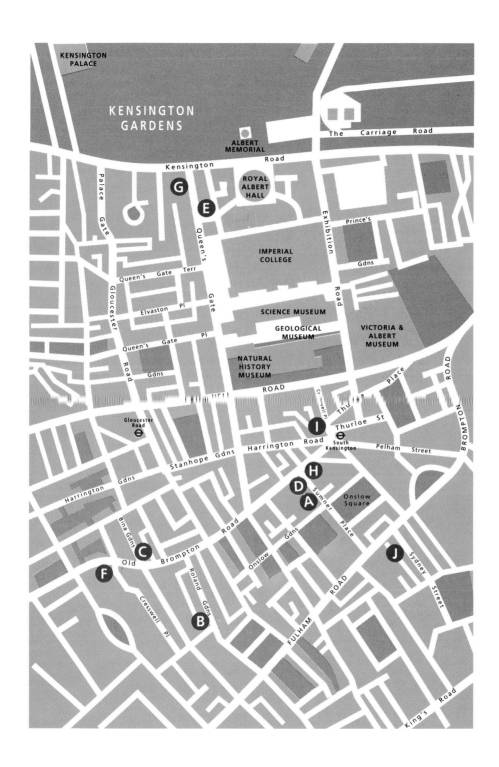

KENSINGTON
PALACE

KENSINGTON
GARDENS

The Carriage Road

ALBERT
MEMORIAL

Kensington   Road

Palace

Gate

G

E

ROYAL
ALBERT
HALL

Exhibition

Prince's

Queen's

Gdns

Gloucester

Queen's Gate Terr

IMPERIAL
COLLEGE

Gate

Elvaston Pl

Road

SCIENCE MUSEUM

GEOLOGICAL
MUSEUM

VICTORIA &
ALBERT
MUSEUM

Queen's Gate Pl

Road

Gdns

NATURAL
HISTORY
MUSEUM

Place

ROAD

ROAD

BROMPTON

Gloucester
Road

Cromwell Pl

Thu

I

Thurloe St

South
Kensington

Harrington Road

Pelham Street

Stanhope Gdns

H

Harrington Gdns

D

A

Sumner

Onslow
Square

Bina Gdns

C

Brompton Road

Onslow

Gdns

Place

J

Sydney Street

Old

F

Roland Gdns

Road

ROAD

Cresswell Pl

B

FULHAM

King's Road

• • • • • • • • •

115

Aster House Hotel

3 Sumner Place London SW7 3EE
Tel 071 581 5888 Fax 071 584 4925

12 rooms, 3 with bath, 9 with shower, telephone, tv, radio on request, refrigerator, safe, ceiling fan and hairdryer on request, no air conditioning • no room service, full buffet breakfast including health food, laundry, dry cleaning • business services, conference rooms • nearest restaurant: Tui • meter parking • no animals • single room £, double room £, suite £, including breakfast, all major credit cards • tube: South Kensington; bus nos: C1, 14, 45, 49, 74, 219

No hotel signs are allowed to spoil the elegant Victorian terrace of Sumner Place, so we looked out for Number Three. This is a privately owned and run bed-and-breakfast hotel built in 1848. Walking up the steps to ring the doorbell, we admired the profusion of plants and flowers flanking the entrance door. A cool, elegant rose marble hall led us to the owner's small office, which doubles as a reception, and leads on to the award-winning back garden. The Aster House has won the London in Bloom competition three years running, and also the British Tourist Authority Bed and Breakfast Award 1988. In addition, it has carried off other trophies in the Brighter Kensington and Chelsea Scheme and the London Newspaper Group Silver

• • • • • • • • • •

Jubilee Challenge, and won the Marjorie Russell Trophy.

The owners have taken immense pleasure and care in decorating the hotel in the English country style. The elegant bedrooms feature canopied beds, and our room had a four-poster, comfortable armchairs, a fireplace and fresh flowers. The standards are high, and the prices amazingly reasonable. We liked the idea of the empty fridge, where we could store drinks of our choice, and were also impressed by the marble bathroom with its stage-lit mirrors.

The Aster House has no lounge, but there is a fabulous conservatory, which they have christened L'Orangerie. Here we found comfy pale pink sofas amid lush palm trees, behind which were tables laid for a buffet breakfast, which is included in the tariff. The buffet featured a good range of healthy foods and some unusual delicacies, such as jam from the Cotswolds. Pots of jam may be purchased as souvenirs. The conservatory is a lovely place to relax and read the newspapers or plan the day ahead.

The house has a no-smoking rule, which health-conscious guests will welcome,

but those who are determined to smoke may do so in the magnificent garden at the back.

Blakes Hotel

33 Roland Gardens London SW7 3PF
Tel 071 370 6701 Fax 071 373 0442 Telex 8813500
Toll free USA 1 800 926 3173

52 rooms, 50 with bath, 2 with shower, air-conditioning in suites and luxury doubles, telephone, satellite tv with CNN, video on request, radio, mini bar, bathrobes, hairdryer, safe, fax in room on request • 24-hour room service, hot and cold snacks, English and Continental breakfast, laundry, dry cleaning • business services, conference facilities for up to 10 in suites • in-house restaurant serving international cuisine • lift, NCP and meter parking • animals welcome by arrangement • single room £££, double room ££££, suite £££–££££, breakfast not included, all major credit cards • tube: Gloucester Road; bus nos: 14, 45, 349

This must be the most extraordinary and unusual hotel in town. We visit often to enjoy the splendour and artistic flair of this establishment and can honestly say it was Blakes Hotel that inspired us to write this book. The owner, Lady Weinberg, the former actress Anouska Hempel, is one of the world's most innovative and creative designers, and this hotel is her showpiece.

From the outside, this stately South Kensington terrace might be just another residential block, but only automatic sliding glass doors separate you from your ultimate fantasy. The foyer with its leather sofas, huge safari umbrella and piles of antique Vuitton travelling trunks is dark and mysterious, highlighted by lavish bunches of unusual and exotic flowers. Even though we have been here many times, every visit brings a new experience, as Ms Hempel is forever creating new scenes for this most theatrical of hotels.

Down the cane staircase, we arrived in the mirrored restaurant with its tables laid in black and white, fresh flowers in big vases and a collection of Southeast Asian clothes and accessories displayed in glass cases on the walls. The food is out of this world. The menu changes seasonally, but favourites like the duck are always available, and this speciality is the best we have ever tasted.

The bedrooms have to be seen to be believed. Who would dream of painting a bedroom black? Blakes has several black bedrooms, with stripped floors stencilled with intricate patterns, walls hung with striking and beautifully framed prints, beds covered in miles and miles of sumptuous silk, four-posters, gilt day beds, carved swan beds.... The Japanese room has a sunken bed. In another room a nineteenth-century Sicilian cabinet forms part of a set including wardrobe and bed.

Everywhere cushions are not just scattered, but heaped. The Library Room has fake books mixed with real ones. Fake book panels cleverly conceal videos, walk-in wardrobes and mini bars. The bathrooms are exquisite, with towels, bathrobes and silk laundry bags to match the colour scheme, and bowls of fragrant pot pourri.

We stayed in the White Room, where everything is white except some natural wood furniture and green plants to break the not-so-cold ice.

If you take a strong fancy to a piece of furniture or any other object you see, you can ask at the desk and, if possible, Ms Hempel will have it copied exactly for you, and shipped to any part of the world. The service is friendly but unobtrusive. We felt looked after, as if a magic hand were making sure that everything was 100 per cent. If ever dreams can become reality, then Blakes is where it will happen.

The Cranley Hotel

8-12 Bina Gardens London SW5 0LA
Tel 071 373 0123 Fax 071 373 9497 Telex 991503

36 air-conditioned rooms, 33 with bath, 3 with shower; kitchenette
(no mini bar), telephone, satellite tv, radio, hairdryer, trouserpress on
request, bathrobes • 24-hour room service, hot and cold snacks •
English and Continental breakfast, laundry, dry cleaning • business
services, safe, no conference room • nearest restaurants: Star of India,
Hilaire • meter parking, lift to third floor only • animals welcome by
arrangement • single room ££, double room ££–££££, suite £££–££££,
breakfast not included, all major credit cards •
tube: Gloucester Road; bus nos: 49, 349

• • • • • • • • • •

The Cranley Hotel is an elegant white building in a quiet residential street in South Kensington and, inside and out, has every appearance of a comfortable private house. The reception desk, for example, is hidden away at the back of a delightful Victorian sitting room. Once run as a bed and breakfast establishment by Albert Einstein's secretary, the hotel has retained many of its original features, thanks to meticulous refurbishment in 1990. Elegant Victorian fireplaces and floor-to-ceiling bay windows are complemented by the owner's imaginative use of colour and fabric to recreate a charming period feel. Wallpaper and hangings are by Osborne & Little, and accessories show clever attention to detail, with books to browse through and fine paintings and furniture to admire.

The Cranley Hotel comprises 36 luxury units, including rooms and several one- and two-bedroomed suites. Instead of the standard mini bar and teasmade, the hotel offers its guests a kitchenette, hidden away behind two panelled doors in the bedroom. This contains a fridge, microwave oven, cooking equipment, china and cutlery. If you prefer, room service offers an interesting menu, and there sre many good restaurants within a stone's throw of the hotel.

The penthouse flat with its patio off the sitting room has views through a remarkable glass wall that take in the Royal Albert Hall, the Natural History and the Victoria & Albert museums. All the bathrooms have luxurious touches, such as Italian ceramic tiles, deep tubs, strong showers, soft white bath towels and robes, and the Garden Suite has the additional attraction of a jacuzzi.

Breakfast can be taken in bed, in the petit salon, or, weather permitting, outside on the patio under large white parasols. Personal service is the hallmark of this charming hotel. The management even provides guests with a leaflet of interesting walks in the area, taking in good places to eat, shop and browse.

Five Sumner Place Hotel

5 Sumner Place London SW7 3EE
Tel 071 584 7586 Fax 071 823 9962

14 rooms with shower, telephone, tv, radio, complimentary mineral water, hairdryer on request, fridges in some rooms • 24-hour room service, hot and cold snacks, English, Continental and buffet breakfast, laundry, dry cleaning • nearest restaurants: Bibendum, Hilaire, San Frediano • lift, meter parking • no animals • single room £–££, double room ££–£££, suite ££, including breakfast, all major credit cards • tube: South Kensington; bus nos: C1, 14, 45, 49, 74, 219

Five Sumner Place Hotel has won the British Tourist Authority's award for the best bed and breakfast in London. Our first impression was of friendly attentive service, immaculately kept and refreshingly uncluttered rooms, and a delightful

• • • • • • • • • •

sense of freedom. Guests are given their own front door key on checking in, so you may come and go as you please, and some rooms are fitted with a small fridge for you to fill with drinks of your choice: we bought ours in a supermarket nearby. Bottled mineral water is provided on the house.

Five Sumner Place is a listed building, a stucco-fronted Victorian terrace in the heart of South Kensington that dates from 1848. Heathrow Airport is 30 minutes away by tube, and the hotel is within easy walking distance of the Natural History Museum, the Science Museum, the Victoria & Albert Museum, the Albert Hall and the famous shops of Knightsbridge and Chelsea.

The bedrooms are traditional in style, and tastefully furnished with graceful drapes. The en suite bathrooms are small, but well appointed. Shower fanatics will have a good time here: there is no need to fiddle endlessly with the hot and cold taps, as each shower is fitted with a temperature gauge.

Five Sumner Place has no restaurant, but room service is available round the clock, and breakfast is really sumptuous. A buffet selection of breakfast foods is

served in the delightful Victorian-style conservatory, where the plants are lovingly tended by the owners. We lingered over aromatic coffee and complimentary newspapers and magazines. Beyond the conservatory is an outdoor terrace, where guests can relax during the summer months.

We found the service at this hotel exemplary and the prices, which include the generous breakfast, extremely reasonable.

The Gore

189 Queen's Gate London SW7 5EX
Tel 071 584 6601 Fax 071 589 8127 Telex 296244

**58 rooms, 35 with bath, 23 with shower, telephone, tv, radio, mini bar,
safe, hairdryer, bathrobes on request, (no air conditioning) • room service,
hot and cold snacks served from 7a.m. – midnight, English and Continental
breakfast, laundry, dry cleaning • business services, conference room •
in-house restaurants: 190 Queen's Gate and Bistro at 190 Queen's Gate •
meter parking, free parking in the park from 11 a.m. until 11 p.m. •
animals welcome by arrangement • single room ££, double room £££,
suite £££, not including breakfast, all major credit cards •
tube: Gloucester Road; bus nos: C1, 9, 10, 52 • closed 24-26 December**

Stepping into this beautiful hotel, which dates from the 1870s, you might imagine
yourself in a florist's or an antiques emporium. The walls are crammed with old
prints in their original frames; to the right, to the left and up the stairs are the most
wonderful tropical palms, which make the foyer look like an extension to the Palm

House in Kew Gardens.

Two spinsters first opened a hotel here in 1908, and now the two grand Victorian terraced houses have been cleverly combined, with a proper regard for nostalgia and without losing any of their original charm.

We were shown a variety of bedrooms, all of them furnished with a great deal of originality. Our favourite was the Venus Room. The furniture here comes from the set of a film starring Judy Garland. Above a comfortable sofa is a painting of Venus; all the features of the room show immaculate attention to period detail.

In the Tudor Room we expected to see Queen Elizabeth I emerge from the bathroom at any moment. The walls are stunningly panelled in dark wood and hung with prints, the working fireplace is decorated with ornamental plates, and as we looked up we discovered a minstrels' gallery and a beamed ceiling. In another room there was an antique four-poster bed and warm sunshine streaming in through a multi-coloured stained glass window.

Our room was newly refurbished; though quite simple, it was full of mellow charm. After having seen so many rag-rolled walls, we found the plain colours refreshing. The bed was large and comfortable, and the walls were hung with interesting prints.

The Green Room at the back of the building is a typical Victorian sitting room. It has a huge fireplace and comfy sofas and armchairs. With its dark green walls and elegant corniced ceiling, this room would be an ideal setting for either afternoon tea or a business meeting.

We enjoyed a pre-dinner drink in the bar while we waited for a table in the busy Bistro at 190 Queen's Gate (tables cannot be booked, but hotel guests are given preference). The bar is a fashionable meeting place. Long and wood-panelled, it has the atmosphere of an international club, and the barmen are as stylish as the clientèle and adept at mixing exotic cocktails. The wait for a table in the buzzing bistro is

justified by the high quality of the food and its reasonable price. Portions are handsome and the dishes are predominantly French and Italian.

Downstairs there is another restaurant called 190 Queen's Gate. Here the atmosphere is more relaxed and the menu more sophisticated. We found both restaurants a stimulating experience and, after a couple of glasses of wine, felt that we were part of a sepia photograph that had come to life.

• • • • • • • • • •

Hotel 167

167 Old Brompton Road London SW5 OAN
Tel 071 373 3221/2 /0672 Fax 071 373 3360

**19 rooms, 11 with bath, 8 with shower; telephone, tv with in-house video
(no radio), teasmade, fridge, shoeshine pack, hairdryer on request • room
service with snacks, Continental buffet breakfast (no laundry or dry
cleaning) • business services, safe, no conference room • nearest restaurants:
Star of India, Mr Wing, Chapter 11 • no lift, NCP and meter parking •
no animals • single room £, double room £, including breakfast;
Visa and Mastercard accepted • tube: Gloucester Road; bus no: 349**

It is always difficult to find a good hotel of character that won't break the budget.
We discovered one in Hotel 167. Occupying a Victorian corner house on the Old
Brompton Road, Hotel 167 is a recently renovated 19-roomed townhouse hotel.

Having admired the overflowing window boxes, we mounted the steps and
entered the beautiful black and white tiled hall. The high ceiling and huge potted
palms are very much in keeping with the Victorian exterior; elsewhere the interior
designer has opted for simplicity. The large reception has plain blinds framed with
grey drapes, a long sweeping desk in cream-painted wood, and a large grey sofa

with black and white cushions. Green plants add a note of freshness throughout the hotel, and there is not a scrap of chintz to be seen anywhere. The reception and lounge doubles as a breakfast room, and the guest can choose from a Continental buffet selection.

No two bedrooms are alike. Some have antique furniture, some modern pine. We saw bentwood rocking chairs, chrome and leather, wicker and black glass, Victorian washstands, Mexican bedspreads, Japanese screens and framed photographs on the walls. However, clutter has no place in this hotel, and Venetian blinds at the windows made a welcome change from the usual heavy drapes. Another unusual touch was the occasional antique in bathrooms, which in most hotels are strictly modern. The beds and bedrooms are spacious, and though some bathrooms have only showers, all are well equipped with towels and toiletries.

Throughout the hotel we found a relaxed atmosphere and cheerful service. This may not be a five-star hotel, but it is certainly extremely good value for money, with breakfast included in the tariff, and the location is excellent. The business traveller will find it most convenient for the exhibition centres at nearby Olympia and Earls Court, the shopper is within a short walk of the King's Road and Fulham Road, and there are many cosmopolitan restaurants in the immediate vicinity. Also close by are the Museum of Natural History, the Science Museum and the Victoria & Albert Museum. Anyone with a penchant for the off-beat will love Hotel 167.

John Howard Hotel

4 Queens Gate London SW7 5EH
Tel 071 581 3011 Fax 071 589 8403 Telex 8813397

40 rooms, 33 with bath, 7 with shower, 12 self-contained apartments, air conditioning, telephone, cable tv, free in-house movies, radio, mini bar, hairdryer, trouserpress, bathrobes • 24-hour room service, hot and cold snacks, English and Continental breakfast, laundry, dry cleaning • business services, safe, conference room • in-house restaurant: The Manor at the Gate, with British and French cuisine • lift, meter parking, free in the park from 11 p.m. to 11 a.m. • no animals • single room ££–£££, double room £££, suite ££, breakfast not included, all major credit cards and JCB • tube: High Street Kensington; bus nos: C1, 9, 10, 49, 52

London is full of elegant tree-lined avenues and Queens Gate is one of them. Here the John Howard Hotel occupies three Regency buildings dating from 1823 adjacent to Kensington Gardens and very close to Hyde Park. It was known as the Portland

• • • • • • • • • •

Hotel until it was bought in the 1970s by Captain John Howard, who renamed it after himself. Captain Howard was a colourful character, a shipping magnate who flourished by trading with China. With the help of his Italian wife Francesca he transformed the hotel into one of London's most stylish venues, introducing full air conditioning well ahead of most other London hotels and, as the *pièce de résistance,* a sushi bar.

When Captain Howard sold, the hotel went into a sad decline, but was restored to its former glory on resale to new owners in 1987. Now, as well as luxuriously appointed rooms, it offers studios and one- and two-bedroomed self-contained apartments with fully equipped kitchens, ideal for longer stays. Some apartments have split-level rooms and are equipped with hi-fi and video. All enjoy daily maid service, and of course guests can still make full use of the hotel's facilities.

The imposing foyer with its arched columns has a cool marble floor, a huge reception desk in exotic wood, and deep royal blue sofas. The grand Regency

bedrooms are lavishly furnished in the traditional style. In the room we saw, pale peach walls were inset with coral panels, and the king-size beds had royal blue valances to match the headboard trims. We also found pickled pine furniture, a private bar and a writing desk. Triple glazing ensures a peaceful night. The bathrooms are spacious, elegant, and well equipped.

Instead of taking the lift to the bar, we walked down the staircase and admired its eighteenth-century tiles. After an apéritif, we were shown to our table in the hotel's restaurant, The Manor at the Gate. The dining room is pretty in peach and pickled pine, and soft background music makes it an intimate venue. The menu is interesting and varied, and the wine list extensive.

Number Sixteen Sumner Place

16 Sumner Place London SW7 3EG
Tel 071 589 5232 Fax 071 584 8615 Telex 266638 SXTEEN

36 rooms, 22 with bath, 14 with shower, telephone, tv (no radio), complimentary mineral water and soft drinks, hairdryer, bathrobes, no air conditioning • honesty bar in lounge (no snacks), English and Continental breakfast, laundry and dry cleaning from Monday to Friday • business services (no conference room), safe • nearest restaurants: Bibendum, Joe's Café • meter parking • no animals or children under 12 • single room £–££, double room ££–£££, suite £££, including Continental breakfast, all major credit cards • tube: South Kensington; bus nos: C1, 14, 49, 74, 219, 503

The passer-by would not guess that behind the immaculate façade of Number Sixteen Sumner Place there lies a small townhouse hotel, as it looks for all the world like a distinguished private residence. The friendly staff checked us in without fuss, and talking to the manageress we were intrigued to discover that she had once been a lady's maid to HRH Princess Anne, now the Princess Royal.

We found the public rooms both elegant and comfortable. In the lounge, with its deep red walls, cream carpet, and rose and soft green armchairs, we were

• • • • • • • • • •

invited to help ourselves to drinks from the honesty bar in the company of the other guests, Americans and some Europeans. The drawing room is bright and sunny with inviting blue sofas and chairs, just the place to curl up with a book or some of the complimentary magazines. In the winter this room is made cosy with a blazing log fire.

The bedrooms are individually furnished. We were offered a choice of three, and picked the pretty Garland Room with its antique furnishings, pink and blue floral drapes and bed canopy, and comfortable seating area. The room was light and spacious and we were served a light breakfast in bed.

We had mid-morning tea in the conservatory and found it a perfect hideaway with its delightful view of the beautifully stocked and colourful garden. It came as no surprise to us to learn that Number Sixteen had won first prize in a competition called A Brighter Kensington and Chelsea and another first in the London in Bloom competition; what did seem extraordinary was to find such a lovely country garden

in the heart of town.

Number Sixteen is conveniently placed for a visit to Christie's – it's fascinating to attend an auction there even if you place no bids. However, we could not pass by the mouthwatering displays in the delicatessens and French patisseries of South Kensington without yielding to temptation.

The Pelham Hotel

15 Cromwell Place London SW7 2LA
Tel 071 589 8288 Fax 071 584 8444 Telex 8814714 TUDOR G

**37 air-conditioned rooms with bath and shower, telephone, satellite tv with
CNN, radio, mini bar, bathrobes, hairdryer, hot-water bottle • 24-hour
room service, hot and cold snacks, English and Continental breakfast,
laundry, dry cleaning • business services, safe, conference room on request •
in-house restaurant: The Pelham, with international cuisine • lift, NCP
parking • animals welcome by arrangement • single room £££, double room
£££, suite £££, not including breakfast, all major credit cards except Diners
• tube: South Kensington; bus nos: C1, B14, 49, 74, 219**

This hotel is part of an early nineteenth-century terrace in the heart of South
Kensington, and opened its doors in 1989 after extensive renovations. It is a
house full of treasures. The first unusual piece of furniture we spotted was the
"conversation seat" in the hall, on which three people can sit back to back; it is
upholstered not in plain velvet but in red and navy check, and gives a clue to the
individual sense of style that runs through the traditional Englishness of this hotel.
  We admired the richness of colours and fabrics throughout the hotel: blue grey
walls ragged with terracotta, a frieze of acorns round the ceiling, acorns on the

tapestry door curtain, acorns on the carved mantelpiece. Everywhere, there is stunning attention to detail and an abundance of gorgeous flowers, both fresh and dried. Wild hedgerow fruits are used in season; you are more likely to find a trail of morning glory than a bunch of chrysanthemums.

The smoking room at the back of the building houses the honesty bar, concealed in a large antique cabinet. The walls here are panelled in dark Brazilian mahogany and the taffeta curtains shimmer blue and green. A chess board stands waiting for a game in this delightful snuggery. Another cabinet full of china and collectables offered many interesting items for sale.

Each of the rooms is individually decorated, with swags of unusual fabrics, sometimes subtle, sometimes verging on the flamboyant, and wonderful touches like antique lace, and silver breakfast services. Some rooms are cosy, others spacious, but the beds are all huge and inviting, with their deep lace-edged pillows and chintz quilts. We stayed in a king-size suite with a luxurious bathroom in grey mottled granite. There were chrome fixtures and fittings and mahogany surrounds. We appreciated the heated towel rails and the jacuzzi bath.

The huge bed had a richly flowered bedspread and canopy and bedside tables heavily draped in checked silk. Our room had French armoires, inside which we found pretty hot-water bottles, and the frilled cream damask curtains were repeated in the lounge, dominated by a vast marble fireplace. We liked the little

side tables with lamps, books, magazines and knick-knacks, and another nice touch was the stencilled frieze of red bows bordering the walls around the ornate ceiling.

Downstairs, the Pelham Restaurant is intimate and cosy. It has its own small bar hung with equestrian prints and with cream and rose patterned sofas surrounding the marble fireplace. In the dining room the theme is fresh – blue, white and pink – and an enormous ornate gold plated mirror hangs above the fireplace.

One of the most novel ideas we found here was a programme of "Special Interest Weeks". Pick your subject from a range including gastronomy, antiques, art, and interior design, and you will be given an itinerary that includes lectures or wine tastings, and visits to stately homes, art galleries and gourmet restaurants, according to choice.

Sydney House Hotel

9-11 Sydney Street London SW3 6PU
Tel 071 376 7711 Fax 071 376 4233

21 rooms, 10 with bath, 11 with shower, telephone with alarm, satellite tv with CNN, radio, mini bar, bathrobes, safe, no air conditioning • 24-hour room service, hot and cold snacks, English, Continental and speciality breakfast, laundry, dry cleaning, cot on request • business services, conference room (holds up to 20) • nearest restaurants: Sydneys, S + P • meter and garage parking • animals on request • single room ££–££££, double room ££–££££, breakfast not included, all major credit cards except Diners • tube: South Kensington; bus nos: 11, 14, 19, 22, 49, 219

In our experience hoteliers normally play safe with décor, deciding upon one easily recognizable traditional style and decorating all their rooms accordingly. Not so the proprietor of Sydney House. As soon as we walked through the doors of this nineteenth-century building, we knew that something different lay in store for us.

The antique reception desk started life in a bank. We remarked on the unusual finish of the walls and were told this was achieved by using an old Venetian

• • • • • • • • • •

technique called *palazzo*. Gold and bronze powders are used as a base, and they shimmer through the green panelling, giving off an almost three-dimensional glow. In one corner of the room is a stone bust on a plinth; the furniture is by Bugatti and the chandelier by Baccarat. We admired the dark green silk brocade sofa and the Indian silver chairs with their delicate leopard print seats.

Our curiosity thoroughly aroused, we were led along dark intimate corridors to the top floor. As each door opened, we journeyed deeper into the world of the imagination. The rooms have names like Royale, Bagatelle, Mexico, Paris, Topkapi, Chinese Leopard, Indian Tiger and Cinderella. Each was as magical as an Aladdin's cave. One room is like a ship's cabin, with porthole windows and an iron four-poster bed draped dramatically in green and black. A door led to the deck: a roof terrace.

We saw a wealth of unique details: a hand-carved and gilded four-poster bed draped in silk brocade, a red tented bed decorated with Parisian monuments, tiger print fabrics and bedspreads, Mexican bedspreads, peacock chairs, wicker sofas, Chinese curtains, Indian carved mirrors and much more.

The Sydney House Hotel deserves an award for its permanent private art exhibition. We saw Hockney etchings in one room, Erté drawings in a corridor, a Miró lithograph in Bagatelle, and a Fragonard ink drawing in Royale.

Downstairs in the breakfast room the sunshine yellow walls show off the dark blue Lloyd Loom furniture to perfection. The unusual wooden shutters are carved to illustrate various foods. The small adjacent bar area is cleverly mirrored to give a spacious feel.

When we complimented him on his stunning décor, the owner told us that he believes a hotel should be full of mystery and intrigue, with dark corridors and explosions of light and colour when you enter the rooms. We can confirm that his unusual approach is a dramatic success.

• • • • • • • • •

Above: Stately trees in Holland Park.

Right: Carnival time in Notting Hill.

• • • • • • • • • •

Holland Park   Notting Hill

Notting Hill is the area lying northwest of Notting Hill Gate. It is bordered to the south by Holland Park Avenue and to the east by Pembridge Villas, and bisected by Ladbroke Grove, an immensely long road that runs from Holland Park Avenue all the way to the Harrow Road. The central streets of Notting Hill run concentrically around Lansdowne Crescent and Stanley Crescent, which form a circle across Ladbroke Grove. Notting Hill has a number of small parks and gardens, and is characterized by elegant nineteenth-century terraced houses. It is a residential area mainly, but also has many interesting and unusual shops, bistros and cafés.

The Ladbroke Estate, as it is known, was laid out from 1850 by Thomas Allom, with large Italianate houses and great expanses of trees. In Kensington Park Road, on its southern boundary, is Kensington Temple, built as a Congregational chapel by John Tarring in 1848. Behind it is the Mercury Theatre, home of the Ballet Rambert, founded in 1926 by Dame Marie Rambert.

One of the major attractions of Notting Hill is the market in Portobello Road. This is open from Monday to Saturday, with a half-day on Thursday. Portobello Road was originally a lane leading to a farm of that name. The name commemorated the capture in 1739 of the exotic Caribbean city of Puerto Bello by Admiral Vernon. The area around Portobello was built up in the 1860s and a market started here about 20 years later. It began with the

basics of fruit and vegetables, and expanded in the 1950s to include antiques, for which it is principally famous today.

The market is liveliest on Saturdays, when it extends for almost a mile. From Chepstow Villas to Lonsdale Road are expensive specialist stalls for collectors. Further down is a mixture of bric-a-brac and ethnic food, especially Caribbean. North of Tavistock Road are stalls with lots of household junk. Under the flyover is a bicycle market, with viewing at noon and an auction at 2 p.m.

Notting Hill is also famous for its carnival, held throughout a summer weekend. This has a distinctly ethnic flavour and is characterized by Caribbean food, music and dancing, and, usually, high spirits and good humour.

Holland House and Holland Park are also worth visiting. Sadly, most of Holland House was destroyed by bombs in 1941, but one wing, an arched loggia and a classical gateway designed by Inigo Jones still remain. The park has woods, a flower garden, a bird sanctuary and an orangery, where music may be heard in summer.

Above: Bargain 'bygones' in Portobello Road market.

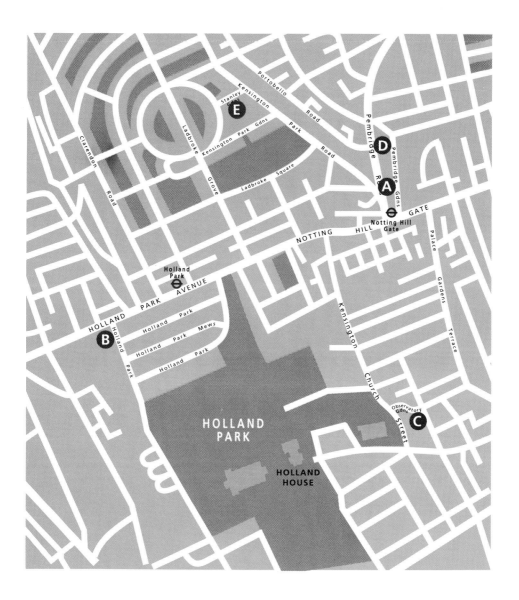

A The Abbey Court

B Halcyon Hotel

C Observatory House Hotel

D Pembridge Court Hotel

E The Portobello Hotel

London Underground

The Abbey Court

20 Pembridge Gardens London W2 4DU
Tel 071 221 7518 Fax 071 792 0858 Telex 262167 ABBYCT

**22 air-conditioned rooms with jacuzzi and shower, telephone, cable tv,
radio, mineral water, shortbread, hairdryer, trouserpress, bathrobes •
24-hour room service, hot and cold snacks, no mini bar, honesty bar
in conservatory, English and Continental breakfast, laundry, dry
cleaning • business services, conference room, safe • nearest restaurant:
Garden Conservatory • NCP and meter parking • no animals or children
under 12 • single room ££, double room ££, suite ££, excluding breakfast,
all major credit cards • tube: Notting Hill Gate; bus nos: 12, 94, 28, 31, 52**

This handsome Victorian mansion in the leafy glades of Notting Hill looks like a
private home and offers the hospitality of a traditional English country residence.
Completely refurbished in 1988, it has been a hotel since 1933, and operating as
The Abbey Court since 1964.

   Friendly staff welcome the visitor into the foyer, papered in deep red and
scented with flowers, which leads to the comfortable lounge and reception area.
Here deep, elegant, chintz-covered sofas and armchairs offer a foretaste of the
standard of furnishing to be met in each room.

• • • • • • • • •

The 22 bedrooms are individually decorated in rich and restful colours – deep blue, dusky pink, rust, gold, cream. The antique furniture gives an exclusive personal touch: period desks and writing tables invite long letters home; generous brass beds and four-posters promise luxurious nights. There are wall stands of Limoges china, well chosen books and magazines, charming old-fashioned radios; and, on bedside tables, mineral water and a tin of shortbread. All the rooms have ample cupboard space. The bathrooms are sumptuous and well equipped with toiletries. They feature Italian marble, gold-plated fittings and heated towel rails. They all have showers as well as whirlpool baths for a relaxing or invigorating soak.

Room service is fast and efficient, and breakfast arrives on china by Villeroy & Boch: moist croissants, aromatic coffee and freshly squeezed orange juice guarantee a good start to the day. Breakfast can also be taken in the newly built conservatory. Here you can sit and relax among a scatter of tapestry cushions and listen to music or enjoy a traditional afternoon tea. An honesty bar offers a selection of drinks and mix-your-own cocktails.

The hotel is within easy walking distance of Portobello Road, famous for its antiques and collectors' market, and of Kensington Church Street, which has a wealth of antique shops and good restaurants.

We were pleased to discover from the owner that a nearby sister hotel to the Abbey Court is being planned, and we look forward to visiting this one in the future.

Halcyon Hotel

81 Holland Park London W11 3RZ
Tel 071 727 7288 Fax 071 229 8516

43 air-conditioned rooms, 40 with bath, 3 with shower; telephone, tv (Sky, CNN, Eurosport), radio, mini bar, hairdryer, bathrobes, safe in most rooms • 24-hour hot and cold snacks, English and Continental breakfast, laundry, dry cleaning • business services, conference rooms • in-house restaurant • lift, NCP parking • no animals • single room ££££, double room ££££, suite ££££, excluding breakfast, all major credit cards • tube: Holland Park; bus nos: 12, 94

The Halcyon Hotel has recently been created out of two nineteenth-century mansions, and only a small brass plaque on the impeccable stuccoed façade reveals that it is no longer a private residence. As we climbed the steps to the entrance, the doors swung open to reveal a Belle Epoque salon in dark green with a fire and antique tapestry-covered chairs.

All the rooms and suites are individually and strikingly designed, and unusually

• • • • • • • • • •

generously proportioned. The Arabian Room is exotic: its walls are painted with desert scenes and its four-poster bed is draped in stripes of gold, blue and green.

We chose a pretty floral room with a four-poster and cleverly angled lighting. The large bathroom was finished in Italian marble with brass fittings and well equipped with Molton Brown toiletries.

The Halcyon Suite has its own conservatory, with rattan furniture and palms, and antique umbrellas suspended from the ceiling. The French boudoir-type bedroom is adorned with pale green wall-to-wall fabric. The lounge has a balcony overlooking quiet gardens at the back.

A few minutes away from the hotel are the Vanderbilt Tennis Club and the Lambton Place Health Club, and health-conscious and sport-minded residents can avail themselves of the facilities of both establishments.

The Halcyon's business services are excellent: translation can be arranged and portable phones are provided on request. There is a one-hour valet service, an in-house video library, and cut flowers grace each room. Staff are dressed in period clothes with cutaway morning coats.

There is a small intimate bar with light oak panelling and comfortable furniture where guests may enjoy a cocktail before dinner in the restaurant. The dining room has large french windows leading to a patio and ornamental garden. The broad-based menu is modern and inventive: the food we chose was of a high standard and surprisingly inexpensive. The restaurant is relaxed: casual dress is fine, the staff are young, energetic and attentive, and after dinner we were treated to an impromptu piano recital in the bar by a flamboyant fellow guest.

Observatory House Hotel

Observatory Gardens 37 Hornton Street London W8 7NR
Tel 071 937 1577 Fax 071 938 3585 Telex 914972 OBSERV G

26 rooms, 4 with bath, 22 with shower; telephone, satellite tv (no radio),
mini bar, teasmade, trouserpress, hairdryer, safe • limited room service with
snacks, English and Continental breakfast, laundry, dry cleaning • business
services, conference rooms on request • nearest restaurants: Clarkes,
Kensington Place, Benedict's, The Churchill; in-house restaurant coming
shortly • NCP and meter parking, no lift • animals welcome by
arrangement • single room £, double room £, breakfast included, all major
credit cards • tube: High Street Kensington, Notting Hill Gate;
bus nos: C1, 9, 10, 12, 27, 28, 31, 49, 52, 70, 94

• • • • • • • • • •

This attractive building a few minutes' walk from Kensington High Street, in a particularly quiet part of the Royal Borough of Kensington and Chelsea, stands on the site of the old Observatory, built by Sir James South in 1831. The late nineteenth-century building is of considerable architectural interest: the same craftsmen worked on the Albert Hall. The original cornicing is particularly stunning. The hotel has recently been refurbished and restaurant facilities had yet to be added at the time of our visit. Traditional English cream teas are another future attraction.

Some of the bedrooms have large bay windows and in all we found a trouserpress, hairdryer, mini bar, tea and coffee making facilities, a personal safe and satellite television. A ground floor room that we visited was notable for its enormous brown marble art deco fireplace. An ornate mirror hangs above it and the room is decorated in pink and blue. It is said to have been used by the late King of Yugoslavia during his exile in this country. A suite on the first floor has a sitting room in the style of a conservatory, with a door leading out to a sunny balcony. In the bedroom there is an alcove with an extra bed in it.

The bathrooms are light and modern, and very well equipped. Most have showers only. The walls are tiled in pale pink, with mirrors set into the tiles, and the floors are marble.

The breakfast room doubles as a sitting room during the day. The centrepiece of this room is a stunning marble fireplace with a gilded mirror hanging above. At breakfast time the tables are brought out and laid with crisp white linen; guests can choose from a generous buffet, with fruit juices, fruit, cheese and cereals. Bacon and eggs, sausage and tomatoes can be cooked to order. Breakfast is included in the hotel's very reasonable tariff.

Pembridge Court Hotel

34 Pembridge Gardens London W2 4DX
Tel 071 229 9977 Fax 071 727 4928 Telex 298363

25 rooms, 17 with bath, 8 with shower, telephone, satellite tv, video on
request, radio, trouserpress, hairdryer, safe, fan on request (air-conditioning
in public areas) • 24-hour room service, hot and cold snacks, English and
Continental breakfast, laundry, dry cleaning • business services, conference
room • in-house restaurant: Caps • lift, parking for two cars • animals
welcome by arrangement • single room ££, double room ££, suite ££,
including full English breakfast, all major credit cards • tube:
Notting Hill Gate; bus nos: 12, 28, 31, 52, 94

• • • • • • • • • •

Have you ever addressed your hotel booking to a cat? Well, try it here. Spencer the ginger tomcat is permanently on duty in the enchanting flower-filled entrance and reception area of The Pembridge Court. This beautiful Victorian house has been developed gradually and lovingly restored over the years into a de luxe townhouse hotel.

Recently a lounge has been added. Here we found pickled ash bookcases full of interesting and colourful books, a Louis XV marble fireplace, bouquets of fragrant blooms, and deep royal blue sofas with blue and cream striped scatter cushions. Lighting can make or break the atmosphere in a room and the owner has chosen carefully: soft lights bring intimacy to this very individual room. A flair for interior decoration is evident all over the hotel.

It took us a long time to climb the stairs, not because we were tired, but because we were fascinated by the incredible collection of Victoriana cleverly displayed in glass frames: purses, dresses, lace collars and fans. There are so many beautiful fans on the walls that the hotel has taken the fan as its motif.

All the bedrooms are individually designed and named after nearby places of interest. We stayed in the Portobello Room (Portobello market is literally on the doorstep). No expense had been spared: the room was spacious, bright and sunny and beautifully decorated, with peach floral curtains and pelmet, and the same window treatment unusually repeated over the bed. A little staircase led to the large bathroom.

In the lift on the way down to the restaurant we were joined by Churchill, the hotel's other ginger tom, who has a liking for this mode of travel. The Pembridge Court's restaurant is called Caps, which was the childhood nickname of the owner, Paul Capra, and there is an amazing display of framed school caps on the walls.

The dinner menu "specials" are written up on a blackboard. The chef produces sumptuous seasonal dishes with unusual combinations of flavour. Most restaurants of this calibre would charge more for such outstandingly good food, and we felt the restaurant was well worth a repeat visit on another trip to town, as it is also open to non-residents via its separate entrance in Pembridge Road.

The staff at the Pembridge Court have been there almost as long as the owner, and have taken the hotel to their heart. Though this was our first visit and we stayed only one night, we were greeted like old friends.

The Portobello Hotel

22 Stanley Gardens London W11 2NG
Tel 071 727 2777 Fax 071 792 9641 Telex 268349 PORT G

25 rooms, 5 with bath, all with shower, some with air conditioning,
all with telephone, tv, radio, mini bar, teasmade, hairdryer • 8 a.m. to
4 p.m. room service, hot and cold snacks, English and Continental
breakfast, laundry, dry cleaning • business services, fax in room on request,
safe, no conference room • small restaurant in house open 24-hours;
nearest restaurant: Julie's • lift, meter parking • animals welcome by
arrangement • single room £, double room ££, suite ££,
breakfast included, all major credit cards •
tube: Notting Hill Gate; bus nos: 28, 31, 52

• • • • • • • • •

Frequented by people who love something out of the ordinary, The Portobello Hotel has a lot to offer. It is situated close to the Portobello antique market and is part of an elegant Victorian terrace built in 1850. Two houses were combined and converted in 1971 to create a privately owned hotel.

The publicity surrounding the opening of this unusual hotel created something of a stir. Here you can sleep in a round bed in the centre of the room, or take a bath in a free-standing brass bathing machine with a maze of brass pipes that could have been designed by Heath Robinson; or you can choose an exquisitely curtained four-poster bed in a room with a painted ceiling. Then there's the Mirror Room at the top of the house, with mirrors everywhere, including overhead. This room also has a sunken bath. The cabin rooms with their mahogany furniture recreate life aboard ship; these rooms are small, but they offer all the usual conveniences and are reasonably priced.

Downstairs a small restaurant and bar is open 24 hours a day. The colour scheme is coral and peach, and it has a truly unique feature: a shell grotto. Thousands of

seashells of all different shapes, sizes and colours have been mounted on the walls. We were delighted by this extraordinary piece of décor.

For gourmets there is another pleasant surprise in store: the owners of The Portobello Hotel also own and run Julie's Restaurant and Champagne Bar, which is just down the road. This is the place where Captain Mark Phillips held his pre-wedding party. On three floors there are several rooms, all with unique character. Julie's Bar has stained glass windows and gothic furniture; then there are the Gothic Room, where you can dine in ecclesiastical splendour, the Gothic Alcove (often used for private parties), the Garden Room with its white spiral staircase and wicker chairs, and the Conservatory, with its glass roof covered in exotic plants.

The hallmarks of The Portobello are originality and informality, and it came as no surprise to us to learn that it has regular clients from the world of pop music. Their identity remains a closely guarded secret of the house. It is said that Tina Turner bought the house next door because she likes The Portobello so much that she uses it as her annexe.

Above: Antiquarian books for sale, Flask Walk, Hampstead.

Right: A summer concert in the grounds of Kenwood House, Hampstead Heath.

Hampstead Swiss Cottage

Hampstead is one of the most desirable residential areas in London. It has a wealth of literary and artistic associations, and was home at one time or another to John Keats, the composer Sir Arthur Bliss, John Middleton Murray and Katharine Mansfield, John Constable, Leigh Hunt and Sigmund Freud. It is characterized by its green spaces, leafy avenues, houses of dignity and character, and exclusive shopping streets with lively boutiques, cafés and restaurants. This is an area with many attractions for both residents and visitors, including Hampstead Village, Hampstead Heath, Parliament Hill, Highgate Village and, if you are prepared to go a little farther afield, Highgate Cemetery.

Beautiful Hampstead Heath is undoubtedly the focal point of the area, with Parliament Hill on its southern extremity affording a magnificently wide view over North London and the City. Further to the east are a series of ponds that lead to Kenwood House, where lakeside concerts are held in summer. Walkers on the Heath will find it hard to believe they are a mere 4 miles from the centre of London.

Hampstead Village has narrow streets that wind up and down the hills. The very attractive houses date predominantly from the nineteenth century, and are now lived in by the academics, artists and media people who give Hampstead its arty reputation. In the eighteenth century, Hampstead Village was a popular spa – the superb terraced houses of Church Row, dating from around 1720, testify to its wealth and importance during this time. You can visit Constable's grave, in the shade of a great cedar tree in the churchyard of St John's in Church Row, and illustrator Kate Greenaway's cottage in nearby Frognal, a fairytale house that must have been an inspiration for her work.

Further south, towards Swiss Cottage, is the Freud Museum, at 20 Maresfield Gardens. Freud took refuge here when the Nazis annexed Austria in 1938, and his daughter Anna has preserved his books, and his collection of Greek, Roman, Egyptian and oriental

antiquities, along with his furniture and personal effects, just as they were in his lifetime.

Visitors exploring Hampstead will not wish to neglect its many fine pubs, including Jack Straw's Castle on North End Way, named after the rebel peasant leader who gathered his supporters here in 1381, and the Bull and Bush, a little further to the north on the same road, which inspired the music hall song. Across the Heath towards Highgate is the Spaniards, an attractive eighteenth-century inn with a toll house that greatly impedes traffic in the rush hour.

Highgate is situated on a twin hill to Hampstead, and has similar charm. A particularly attractive feature is the romantically wild cemetery, with its gothic chapels and Egyptian catacombs crumbling and overgrown with ivy. Many famous people are buried here, including Michael Faraday, Sir Rowland Hill, George Eliot, Christina Rossetti, Herbert Spencer and John Galsworthy. Perhaps the most famous Highgate grave is that of Karl Marx, who died in Hampstead in 1883; it lies in the newer eastern part of the cemetery.

Above: Well Walk, Hampstead.

Right: The City of London seen from Hampstead.

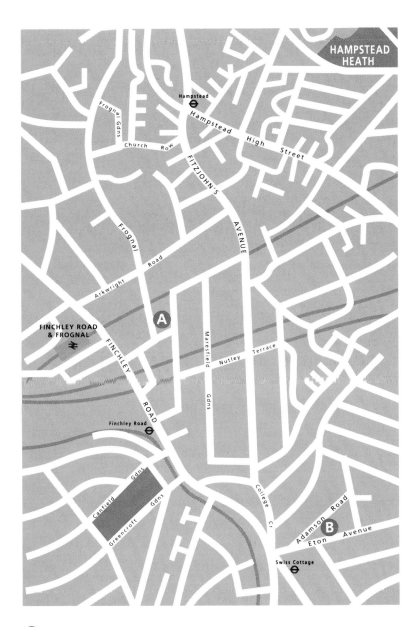

Ⓐ The Langorf

Ⓑ Swiss Cottage Hotel

⊖ London Underground

⇌ British Rail

The Langorf Hotel

20 Frognal London NW3 6AG
Tel 071 794 4483 Fax 071 435 9055

32 rooms, 26 with bath, 6 with shower; telephone, satellite tv, radio, teasmade (no mini bar) hairdryer • 24-hour room service, hot and cold snacks, Continental breakfast, laundry, dry cleaning • business services, safe, conference room on request • nearest restaurant: Mamma Rosa • lift, parking • no animals • single room £, double room £, including breakfast, all major credit cards and En Route • tube: Finchley Road; bus no: 113

Tucked away discreetly in a quiet residential street called Frognal, a few minutes' walk away from Hampstead village, is this delightful Edwardian residence. Totally refurbished in 1990, it is now an elegant townhouse hotel.

A striking black and white tiled path and steps lead to the front door. Inside we found an attractive blue and white lounge and reception area with dark blue leather chesterfields and floral curtains. Leading off from this is the spacious and airy breakfast room and bar, which reminded us of a French bistro. The buffet-style breakfast is extremely good value as it is included in the very reasonable hotel tariff. Guests can choose from melon and other fresh fruits, and there is a variety

• • • • • • • • • •

of cheeses as well as freshly baked croissants, tea and coffee and other more conventional breakfast foods. Large French windows lead out to a leafy, gently sloping garden, and in the evening this lovely room doubles as a cocktail lounge.

The hotel does not have a restaurant, but there are many interesting places to eat nearby, and the Langorf has special arrangements with two of them so that residents' bills can be charged directly to their hotel account.

The bedrooms are uniform in their décor, with soft coral furnishings, padded bedheads and silver grey bedspreads. The rooms are bright and airy, with brilliant white-tiled private bathrooms of the highest quality. We particularly appreciated the high-pressure showers. Remote-control television, central heating, direct-dial telephones, and good coffee and tea making facilities all added to our comfort.

One of the attractions of staying here is the proximity of Hampstead village; in the High Street you will find many fashionable boutiques and restaurants. No one should miss a walk on Hampstead Heath, with its many acres of wild and unfenced parkland. On a clear day St Paul's Cathedral may be glimpsed in the distance; this is the view painted by John Constable. For music lovers there is Kenwood, a beautiful mansion full of antiques and paintings by Reynolds and Angelica Kauffmann. On summer evenings there are open-air concerts beside the lake at Kenwood.

Swiss Cottage Hotel

4 Adamson Road London NW3 3HP
Tel 071 722 2281 Fax 071 483 4588 Telex 297232 SWISCO G

80 rooms, 69 with bath, 11 with shower; 17 apartments, telephone, tv, radio, trouserpress, hairdryer on request (no air conditioning) • 24-hour room service, hot and cold snacks, English breakfast, laundry, dry cleaning • business services, conference rooms, safe • in-house restaurant serving English and international cuisine • lift, parking • no animals • single room ££–£££, double room ££–£££, apartments £–££, including full English breakfast, all major credit cards • tube: Swiss Cottage; bus nos: 13, 31, 113

In the 1930s this hotel was opened as a home for refugees on the strength of a perfectly baked Sacher Torte. The philanthropic owners took the cake to their bank manager, who promised them an overdraft as long as they provided him with an equally delicious cake every Christmas.

• • • • • • • • • •

In 1964 the four Victorian houses that comprise the hotel changed hands and underwent extensive renovation. The establishment was named The Swiss Cottage Hotel and filled with antique furniture, rugs and paintings.

Checking in, we discovered a most unusual reception desk: a marble-topped cabinet inlaid with mother-of-pearl, displaying a collection of Staffordshire figurines. The splendid Victorian-inspired sitting room has a Blüthner boudoir grand piano, occasionally played by visiting concert pianists. The hotel also has a bar and spacious conference facilities.

This is a family-run hotel, and guests are made to feel at home. The bedrooms display a delightfully old-fashioned individual character: ours had a huge mirrored wardrobe inlaid with marquetry that offered ample storage space, and a charming antique writing desk.

A special feature of the Swiss Cottage Hotel is its 14 apartments, designed for extended stays. These offer all the privacy of your own town flat in a superb location, combined with the amenities of a first-rate hotel. There are studio, one-bedroom and two-bedroom apartments, suitable for up to four guests, and all have private bathroom and kitchen facilities and their own front door key. The very

reasonable tariff includes full English breakfast in the hotel and the apartments are serviced twice a week.

The hotel is surrounded by a most charming garden. Guests can stroll through the secluded courtyard or relax under the vine-draped pergola. We thought it a delightful place to stay.

Above: The Thames at dawn, with Hammersmith Bridge in the background.

Right: Tiling on the Michelin building in Fulham Road.

West Kensington   Earls Court   Fulham

Fulham is situated in a bend on the River Thames opposite Putney and Barnes, with West Kensington to the northwest and Earls Court to the northeast. Earls Court occupies an area between the Cromwell Road and the Old Brompton Road, with the Earls Court Exhibition Centre as its main landmark. West Kensington is bordered to the north by the Hammersmith Road and to the west by the Warwick Road.

Fulham was once famous for its market gardens. In 1671 John Dwight established a pottery in New King's Road where Fulham stoneware was made. A nineteenth-century bottle kiln was discovered there in 1975. Beyond Putney Bridge Station, at the junction of New King's Road and Fulham High Street, is Ranelagh Gardens, leading to the fashionable Hurlingham Club. This was founded in 1869 in a house built around 1760, and in 1954 part of the extensive gardens was converted into a public park with an athletics stadium. Fulham Indoor Market, on the North End Road, is open on Saturdays.

The parish church of Fulham is All Saints' Church, which dates from 1886 and can be found near the north end of Putney Bridge. There is a fifteenth-century tower and, inside, sixteenth-century brass and many monuments from the seventeenth century. Part of Fulham Palace dates from the early sixteenth century. The site was owned by the Bishopric of London

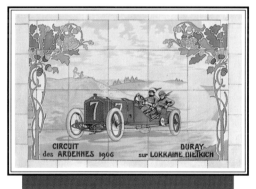

CIRCUIT
des ARDENNES 1906

DURAY
sur LORRAINE DIETRICH

from about 691, and the palace remained the residence of the Bishop of London until 1973. Its moat is now a public garden. Between the palace grounds and the river is Bishop's Park. Fans gather on the terrace here to watch the start of the Oxford and Cambridge Boat Race.

Just off the Earls Court Road is Bolton Gardens, where Beatrix Potter lived as a girl. Nearby Earls Court Square is the home of the Poetry Society, founded in 1909. The Earls Court Exhibition Centre in Warwick Road, designed by C. Howard Crane, was completed in 1937. At the time, it was the largest reinforced concrete structure in Europe. In 1989 a second exibition area, Level 2, was opened, and this huge complex houses all kinds of events and trade shows.

• • • • • • • • • •

Above: The Thames at Barnes.

Lillie Road is the site of Earls Court's Sunday morning market. It sells general household goods and budget clothes, along with an excellent selection of good quality fabrics and electrical goods.

West Kensington is the home of the area's other major exhibition centre, Olympia. On the junction of Hammersmith Road and Olympia itself, the centre plays host to various exhibitions throughout the year, most famously the Ideal Home Exhibition, which takes place in March. Hammersmith Road is the site of St Paul's School, a public school now moved to Barnes, but which became Field-Marshal Lord Montgomery's headquarters during the planning of the 1944 invasion of Normandy.

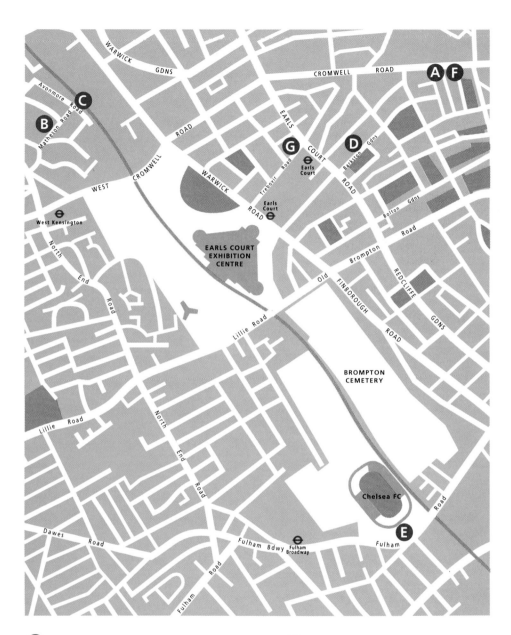

Ⓐ Adelphi Hotel

Ⓑ Aston Court Hotel

Ⓒ Avonmore Hotel

Ⓓ The Burns Park Hotel

Ⓔ La Reserve

Ⓕ The Park International Hotel

Ⓖ Rushmore Hotel

⊖ London Underground

Adelphi Hotel

127-129 Cromwell Road, London SW7 4DT
Tel 071 373 7177   Fax 071 373 7720   Telex 8813164 ADELFI G

70 rooms, 65 with bath, 5 with shower; telephone, cable tv, radio, (no mini bar or teasmade), trouserpress, hairdryer • 24-hour room service, hot and cold snacks, English and Continental breakfast, laundry, dry cleaning • business services, safe, 3 conference rooms • nearest restaurants: The Bombay Brasserie, Le Quai St Pierre • lift, NCP and meter parking • animals welcome by arrangement • single room ££, double room ££, breakfast not included, all major credit cards, including JCB • tube: Gloucester Road; bus nos: 49, 74, Airbus

This elegant red-brick Victorian building is situated on the corner of Cromwell Road with easy access from Heathrow and into the West End. The hotel is privately owned. It was refurbished and redecorated in 1990 and offers very good value for money.

The reception is panelled in English rosewood and the friendly staff were most helpful on our arrival. The colour scheme in the reception is blue and pink, and there is a small but comfortable seating area.

The foyer leads into the large high-ceilinged lounge. This room has huge bay windows and beautifully painted ornate cornicing. The cream-dragged walls are flanked with red leather banquette seats, and there are also red tub chairs and red

and cream striped sofas. The rosewood occasional tables were imported from China.

Next we walked through to the well stocked bar, spacious enough to hold a private conversation in without being overheard.

The 70 bedrooms vary slightly in size and shape but the décor is uniform throughout, being mainly blue with multicoloured curtains and matching bedspreads. The furniture is in rosewood and there is ample storage space. Some rooms have a large bay window or a small balcony; all are provided with a hairdryer and a trouserpress. The bathrooms are very modern, tiled in blue and pink, and well equipped with toiletries. The mirrors are well lit, and the bath panels and toilet seats are of wood.

Downstairs in the basement is the Conservatory Restaurant. Sunshine streams in through a large skylight onto cheerful yellow walls. When we visited the hotel it served breakfast only, but we were told of plans to open in the evening for dinner in the not-too-distant future. There are also numerous good restaurants within easy walking distance of the hotel.

The Adelphi is very reasonably priced and well furnished, though not quite so sumptuously appointed as many of the boutique hotels nearby. It is conveniently located in a neighbourhood with a delightful village atmosphere and offers three conference rooms for business meetings.

Aston Court Hotel

25–27 Matheson Road London W14 8SN
Tel 071 602 9954 Fax 071 371 1338 Telex 919208 ASTON G

29 rooms, 13 with bath, 16 with shower; telephone, satellite tv, radio, mini bar, teasmade, trouserpress, hairdryer, iron, bathrobes • 24-hour room service, cold snacks round the clock, hot snacks until 11.30 p.m., English and Continental breakfast, laundry, dry cleaning • business services, safe, conference room • nearest restaurants: Belvedere, Cibo • lift, free parking • single room £, double room £, suite £, breakfast included, all major credit cards • tube: West Kensington; bus nos: 9, 10, 27, 28, 33, 49

This privately owned hotel was completely redeveloped and refurbished in 1989. It looks from the outside like a large private house and is situated in a quiet tree-lined residential street in West Kensington.

An unusual feature in the entrance is a large ceramic leopard. The reception and lounge leads to the bar and breakfast room and the colour scheme is soothing: peaches and cream. We noticed pickled pine furniture and a selection of Spy cartoons on the walls.

The bedrooms vary in spaciousness, though all are uniformly decorated and furnished. Special features are direct-dial telephones, bathrobes, trouserpresses, irons and hairdryers. The bathrooms have pink marble tiles and are well equipped

• • • • • • • • • •

with a good supply of toiletries and large white towels.

Returning to the hotel from a visit to the theatre, we joined other guests in a cocktail and some lively conversation at the bar. Our companions turned out to be exhibiting at the antiques fair round the corner at Olympia; they were particularly pleased with the hotel's convenient location and the fact that parking is free.

Breakfast is included in this hotel's very reasonable tariff, and we enjoyed excellent bacon and eggs in the light and pleasant Conservatory Room.

Although this is a small hotel, it offers excellent services for the business traveller, including full conference facilities and secretarial services on request. The staff gave us friendly and unobtrusive service, and advised us of good places to eat nearby. One that we discovered was Rolling Stone Bill Wyman's restaurant, Sticky Fingers.

This is a convenient location, as the hotel is only a few minutes' walk from Kensington High Street, with its wide range of boutiques and shops, and from Holland Park, a beautiful place for an early morning jog. Don't miss the art shows

in Holland Park's Orangery; they change every month.

Avonmore Hotel

66 Avonmore Road London W14 8RS
Tel 071 603 3121/4296 Fax 071 603 4035 Telex 945922 (ATTN K357)

9 rooms, 4 with bath, 5 with shower; telephone, tv, radio, fridge with
soft drinks, alarm clock, hairdryer and iron on request • room service
with snacks until midnight, free tea and coffee all day, English and
Continental breakfast, laundry, dry cleaning • business services, safe,
no conference room • nearest restaurants: Al Gallo d'Oro, Avallioni •
no lift, free parking • no animals • single room £, double room £,
including English breakfast, no credit cards accepted •
tube: West Kensington; bus nos: 9, 10, 27, 28, 33, 49

• • • • • • • • • •

A guesthouse since 1927, this hotel was taken over by the current owners nine years ago. They have recently refurbished the elegant Victorian building to the highest standard, and although the Avonmore is less glamorous than some of the other hotels featured in this book, we found it pleasantly decorated and furnished and extremely good value for money. Staff and proprietor gave us a warm welcome and we found them friendly and helpful.

Situated in a quiet residential street in West Kensington, the hotel is about 15 minutes by taxi from the West End.

From the reception, we were shown through into the breakfast room and bar, which is decorated in soft peach and limed oak. There were pretty posies of dried flowers on all the tables. The proprietor also offers free tea and coffee all day long, and this can be taken downstairs or brought to your room. We enjoyed our full English breakfast with fellow residents, and the proprietor introduced us all to each other, ensuring a friendly atmosphere and lively conversation.

The bedrooms are decorated in peach and blue, and our beds had attractive scatter cushions. All rooms have en suite bathrooms. The bathrooms are tiled in blue, peach or green and fitted with strong showers, sometimes in a separate cabinet. Some rooms have showers only, but all bathrooms are of modern design.

The Avonmore Hotel has won the AA National Award for the best private hotel in London, which came as no surprise to us. It is very popular with business travellers as well as tourists. We were particularly impressed by the care the proprietor took to make guests feel at home; on one occasion we noticed her take out a map and sit down to explain some detail of London geography to a stranger to the city.

• • • • • • • • •

The Burns Park Hotel

18–26 Barkston Gardens London SW5 OEN
Tel 071 373 3151 Fax 071 370 4090 Telex 27885 BURNS G

**106 rooms with bath, telephone, satellite tv, radio, teasmade (no mini bar),
hairdryer, trouserpress • room service with hot and cold snacks from
7 a.m. to 11 p.m, English and Continental breakfast, laundry, dry
cleaning • business services, safe, 2 conference rooms • in-house restaurant
and bar • lift, meter parking • no animals except guide dogs • single
room ££, double room ££, breakfast not included, all major credit
cards • tube: Earls Court; bus nos: C3 31, 74, 349**

This elegant Victorian hotel overlooks a peaceful residential square in Earls Court
and is a stone's throw from the international exhibition centres Olympia and Earls
Court. It was completely refurbished in 1989 and meets the high standards the
modern traveller has come to expect. The blue plaque outside commemorates the
fact that the actress Ellen Terry once lived here; the foyer is said to have been her
dining room. Today the foyer is a grand reception area with a floor in black and
peach marble, and walls panelled in yew. It looks out on to a tree-lined road over
window boxes bursting with flowers.

The hotel has several decorative schemes for its bedrooms, and we slept in a

• • • • • • • • • •

room with pretty paisley curtains and matching bedspread, comfortable tub chairs and a sofa. The colours revolved around rust red. There was an ample writing desk, and the walls were hung with Dufy prints. We were invited to take a look in other bedrooms and found them similarly well appointed; some were decorated in blue, others in peach. Our bathroom was finished in bright tiles with a dark grey frieze, and we had a good supply of toiletries and generously sized towels.

The Tulip Bar on the ground floor is small and intimate in warm peach. There are comfortable tub chairs, like those in the bedrooms, and the walls are hung with prints. The windows overlook the hotel's lovely gardens, which are open to residents. Descending a few steps from the bar, we came to the restaurant, which is light and airy, with cane chairs and lots of mirrors on the walls. During the summer months the doors to the terrace are left open and tables are set outside for *al fresco* dining and barbecues.

La Reserve

422-428 Fulham Road London SW6 1DU
Tel 071 385 8561 Fax 071 385 7662

41 rooms with bath and shower, telephone, satellite tv, radio, mini bar,
teasmade, hairdryer, trouserpress • 24-hour room service, hot and cold
snacks, Continental breakfast, laundry, dry cleaning, no air conditioning •
business services, conference room, safe • in-house restaurant • lift, nearby
parking • animals welcome by request • single room ££, double room ££,
suite £, breakfast included, all major credit cards •
tube: Fulham Broadway; bus no: 14

We had heard from friends about La Reserve's imaginative restaurant before we made our booking. The dining room is stylishly decorated in black and white, with large ornamental plates on polished wooden tables and conical vases mounted on the walls. The awkward-looking chairs turned out to be very comfortable indeed. The modern menu shows a strong Thai and oriental influence and uses only fresh produce. We can highly recommend it.

Adjoining the dining room is the fashionable cocktail bar with its striking off-beat furniture. Here the black and white theme continues, relieved by splashes of vivid colour. The ceiling features an unusual star light design. One or two oil lamps stand on a large frosted glass coffee table. There is a refreshing lack of clutter. The bar is divided from the lounge by a free-standing working fireplace encased in glass. The floor covering is not carpet but Junkers ship deck flooring. The sofas, in black with cushions in flat vivid colours, are reminiscent of Mondrian. The public rooms are hung with paintings by up-and-coming young artists which are replaced every few weeks.

The bedrooms too show the owner's considerable flair for colour and line, and the simplicity of the furniture, much of it from the French company Ligne Roset, is complemented by the unfussy window treatments. Our room had twentieth-century prints, modern grey headboards and grey and mauve bedspreads. In other rooms we saw tones of burnt orange, beige and rust. The generous bathrooms are supplied with toiletries that have not been tested on animals. There is a private garden in the Japanese style, with a small terrace and tables.

The hotel is affordably priced, and only 15 minutes by taxi from the West End. There are lots of interesting boutiques and antique shops within easy walking distance.

• • • • • • • • •

The Park International Hotel

117-125 Cromwell Road London SW7 4DS
Tel 071 370 5711 Fax 071 244 9211 Telex 296822 KEN G

117 rooms, 105 with bath, 12 with shower; telephone, satellite tv, radio, teasmade (no mini bar), hairdryer, trouserpress, some jacuzzis • room service with hot and cold snacks from 7 a.m. to 11 p.m, English and Continental breakfast, laundry, dry cleaning • business services, safe, air-conditioned conference room • in-house restaurant: Park Grill • lift, NCP and meter parking • no animals • single room ££, double room ££, breakfast not included, all major credit cards • tube: Gloucester Road; bus nos: 74, 49, Airbus

• • • • • • • • • •

This hotel occupies a listed Victorian building in the Royal Borough of Chelsea and Kensington. Comprising five adjoining houses, it was completely refurbished in 1988 to the highest international standards. The imposing white façade is decorated with window boxes full of flowers, and there is a large and welcoming reception area that doubles as a lounge. The colour scheme here is peach and blue, and the wood is pickled pine. The walls are hung with colourful prints and comfortable seating is arranged in the glow of brass lamps.

The light and airy bar room has a huge oak-panelled bar and cane bar stools. The walls are attractively sponged, and tub chairs are grouped around wooden tables. The barman is a fantastic mixer of drinks and, for good measure, dispenses good advice on London's Sunday markets.

Like the bar, the Park Grill is also open to non-residents. The colour scheme is again peach and blue, with peach table linen and fresh flowers on all the tables. The menu is small, and the chef specializes in grills, as the name of the restaurant suggests. We ate smoked salmon followed by tournedos. The wine list is interesting, with a particularly good selection of French wines. We also liked the room service menu, which features dishes such as vegetable lasagne and chicken and mushroom pancakes. In the restaurant, as elsewhere, the staff were friendly and helpful.

The Park International has the same decorative scheme in all its bedrooms, though the bigger executive rooms have the additional luxury of a jacuzzi. The hotel's colours of peach and blue are repeated in the bedrooms, and the bedspreads and curtains are in a paisley print. In the executive rooms there is also a comfortable sitting area with deep blue chairs and sofa.

We enjoyed having a control panel by the bed from which we could operate the television and lights. Another good feature was a full-length mirror on the wall. The bathrooms are tiled and decorated with a small frieze. Ours was well equipped with plenty of large fluffy towels and toiletries.

Air conditioning is available only in the conference room, which seats up to 45 people and caters for private dinner parties as well as business meetings.

We found the hotel conveniently located – with the tube station nearby it took only 15 minutes to get to Piccadilly. Joggers will enjoy running up to Kensington Gardens for some early morning exercise.

• • • • • • • • •

Rushmore Hotel

11 Trebovir Road London SW5 9LS
Tel 071 370 3839 Fax 071 370 0274 Telex 297761 Ref 1933

22 rooms, all with shower, 8 with bath; telephone, satellite tv with Sky, CNN, MTV, Eurosport (no radio), teasmade (no mini bar), hairdryer on request • Continental breakfast, laundry, dry cleaning, no room service • business services, conference rooms, safe • nearest restaurants: Lou Pescadou, La Primula, Ponte Vecchio, Crystal Palace • parking, no lift • animals welcome by arrangement • single room £, double room £, including breakfast, all major credit cards, no Diners • tube: Earls Court; bus nos: C3, 30, 31, 74, Airbus

This hotel is situated in a quiet side street in the Royal Borough of Kensington and Chelsea away from the hustle and bustle of Earls Court. The rooms here are stylishly decorated and exceptionally good value for money. The private owner has taken great pride in renovating what looks from the outside like an ordinary small Victorian hotel, with the help of a renowned international interior designer.

The façade of the hotel is prettily decorated with window boxes and we

• • • • • • • • • •

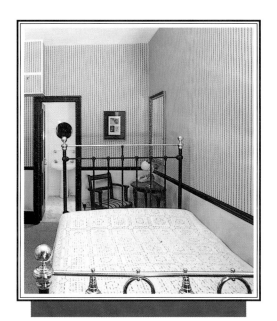

climbed the grey marble steps into the foyer. We seemed to be entering the set of an Italian opera. Our eyes took in a sweeping reception desk, natural stone flooring, burnt sienna walls and a mural depicting the hills of Tuscany.

Our exploration of the rooms revealed some unusual design ideas. There is no lift, so we climbed the stairs to the fourth floor, where we found very spacious attic rooms with sloping ceilings and skylight windows. The Japanese room had a large ornamental fan mounted on the wall and a bamboo bedstead; there was an elegant Edwardian room with gold stencilling and ornate grey-painted wall mouldings; and the black and gold "safari" room had a mosquito net above the bed and original shutters. In the Ocean Room there were huge pictures of exotic beaches, azure walls and ship's cabin-type furniture. The Laura Ashley rooms had delightful country prints and chintz curtains.

Most of the bathrooms are in marble; some have showers only, but all are modern and well equipped. The hotel's breakfast room has dusky pink drapes and while you are eating your Continental breakfast you can admire another mural,

which gives the illusion of looking out of a window onto rolling hills.

Business people will appreciate the closeness of the exibition centres at Earls Court and Olympia, and the extensive business facilities the hotel offers, including multilingual staff and secretarial services.

There is no restaurant here, but Chinese, Indian, Italian, Greek and French food can all be found only a few minutes' walk away.

The Rushmore Hotel has lots of flair, is efficiently run, and is a great bargain.

Wimbledon Richmond Ealing Heathrow

The names of three of these four west-of-London locations will probably be familiar to the visitor. Wimbledon is world famous for the All England Club's lawn tennis championships, held in the middle two weeks of June. Spectators come here to enjoy traditional strawberries-and-cream teas, as well as to watch the top tennis stars compete for this most prestigious of trophies. Wimbledon also has a delightful park, a common with horse riding, and two golf courses. Richmond is known for its fine houses and its deer park; and Heathrow for its international airport.

Ealing, situated off the Western Avenue, the A40 approach to London from High Wycombe, Oxford and South Wales, is less well known, but it too has its attractions: leafy boulevards; a number of parks and sports grounds, including the Ealing Cricket Club; the medieval Greenford Church with its timber tower; and two early nineteenth-century mansions, Gunnersbury Park and Pitshanger Manor, which is now a museum. Ealing Broadway is a busy shopping thoroughfare with a tube station that provides direct access to the West End.

All visitors to the west of London will find plenty to attract them to Richmond. The connection between Richmond and royalty began in 1125 when Henry I built the Palace of Sheen. In 1499 a great fire devastated this building and Henry VII rebuilt it, naming it Richmond Palace from his former title, Earl of Richmond (the original Richmond is in Yorkshire). Henry VII died in Richmond Palace, and in 1603 so did his even more illustrious descendant, Elizabeth I. In 1634 Charles I evacuated his court to Richmond Palace during a plague, but he was the last monarch to live there and after his residence the palace gradually fell into decay.

What little remains of this once splendid edifice can be seen on the western side of Richmond Green. Here you will find a Tudor gatehouse and, within, private houses. These were built later and some incorporate parts of the palace's original brickwork. The Trumpeters House is of particular note because of its fine eighteenth-century pedimented façade.

Exceptionally fine eighteenth- and nineteenth-century houses border Richmond Green on all sides. Maids of Honour Row was built in 1724 for the ladies in waiting to Caroline, later queen to George II, who at that time lived nearby in Kew.

Richmond Park comprises over 2,000 acres and was first enclosed by Charles I. Today it is still a royal park, and London's best preserved area of countryside. Protected herds of red and fallow deer roam here, and the

heath and woodland are notable for a large variety of other indigenous animals, birds and plants.

Just north of Richmond Park across the A316, the Twickenham Road, is another of London's famous green areas: the Royal Botanic Gardens at Kew. These gardens are open daily during daylight hours (closing time in summer is as late as 8 p.m, and in winter as early as 3.30

Far left: The Thames at Richmond.

Left: Kew Gardens' famous Chinese pagoda.

p.m). Here you will find a collection of plants and trees unrivalled anywhere in the world. Despite the devastations of the 1987 hurricane, Kew is still a magnificent experience, with delightful walks and beautiful views.

The botanic gardens were founded in 1759 in the grounds of two royal residences: Richmond Lodge and the White House. They owe much of their splendour to Sir Joseph Banks, who sailed with Captain Cook to the South Seas and sent young botanists all over the world in quest of specimens.

Above: A view across Richmond Park.

A Cannizaro House

B MV Captain Webb

C The Petersham Hotel

D The Richmond Gate Hotel

E 52 Mount Park Road

London Underground

British Rail

Wimbledon

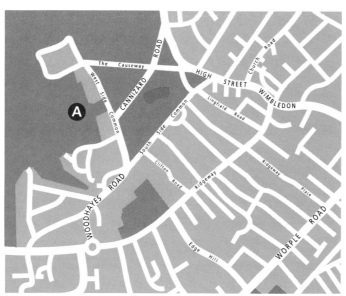

Richmond

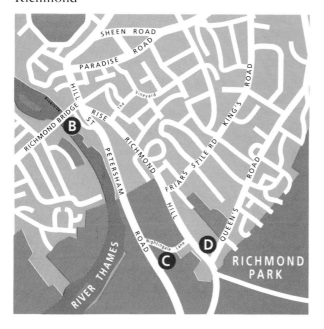

Ealing

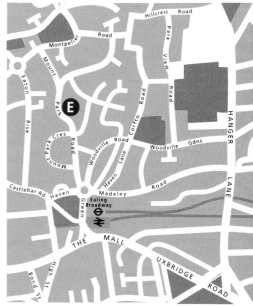

Cannizaro House

West Side Wimbledon Common London SW19 4UF
Tel 081 879 1464 Fax 081 879 7338 Telex 9413837

**46 en-suite rooms with telephone, tv, in-house movies, radio, hairdryer,
trouserpress, bathrobes, no air conditioning • 24-hour room service,
hot and cold snacks (no mini bar), English and Continental breakfast,
laundry, dry cleaning • business services, 4 conference rooms, safe •
in-house restaurant with modern cuisine • lift, free parking • animals
welcome by arrangement • single room ££, double room ££–£££,
suite £££, excluding breakfast, all major credit cards •
limousine service; tube: Wimbledon**

Imposing Cannizaro House was built in 1705 by a wealthy London merchant,
William Browne, and as a private home it attracted visitors such as Prime Minister
William Pitt, and in the nineteenth century Oscar Wilde, Alfred Lord Tennyson,
Henry James and the Prince and Princess of Wales. After major restoration it
opened as a hotel in June 1987.

    The Georgian mansion is London's first country house hotel, set in the 34 acres
of Cannizaro Park on the edge of Wimbledon Common. Though central London is
only a few miles away in the hotel's limousine, the grounds are a haven of
tranquility, with sweeping lawns, a gothic aviary, an ornamental lake and a
magical sunken garden.

• • • • • • • • • •

The splendour of Cannizaro House strikes the visitor immediately on entering the magnificent central room which is dominated by an ornate marble fireplace decorated with cherubs, where a log fire blazes in the winter months. The subdued elegance of the furnishings allows the eye to feast on the rich colours of the painted ceiling, where more cherubs cavort among the gods. Here you may sit, with a view over the park, and take tea before ascending the grand staircase to the bedrooms.

The Cannizaro's spacious suites are characterized by interesting and individual lines, tall windows and stately views, fine furniture and accessories, and rich fabrics. Deep comfort and discreet luxury are the hallmarks of this sumptuous hotel. Each room is fragrant with flowers and pot pourri, the toiletries are by Potter & Moore, some of the bathrooms have double washbasins, all have robes, and if you put your shoes outside the door at night, they'll be waiting for you gleaming in the morning.

The honeymoon service includes a suite with a four-poster bed, flowers, fruit and champagne on arrival, an intimate dinner, full English breakfast and limousine transfer to Heathrow or Gatwick airport. For the business traveller there is a selection of conference rooms with secretarial services, and private dining rooms. Clients can be entertained to lunch in the oak-panelled boardroom with its splendid carved overmantel. In June the hotel makes an ideal base from which to visit the Wimbledon Tennis Championships.

The restaurant at Cannizaro House offers an imaginative menu that changes every day and features seasonal delicacies such as game and shellfish. Bread and

preserves are made on the premises, in true country house style. There are around 270 wines in the cellars, predominantly French and German, and extra time should be allowed when choosing from the wine list. An additional attraction of eating here is that guests are entertained by a very talented pianist.

MV Captain Webb

The Landing Stage Riverside Richmond on Thames Surrey TW10 6UJ
Tel 0836 202408

7 cabins with shower • berths for up to 12 guests with dinner or buffets for 40 guests • restaurant serves English food made to historic recipes • air conditioning • lounge with tv, radio and bar • telephone on board, limited business services • can accommodate a conference of up to 12 people • can collect guests from different riverside locations • may only be chartered: £550 for a cruising lunch or dinner for 12, or a buffet for 40; £990 for dinner, bed and full English breakfast for 12; Visa, Diners, Amex

The MV Captain Webb is a floating hotel: an ingeniously converted 100-year-old Dutch clipper barge. The private parties and business executives who charter this 31-metre motor vessel for a cruise up the Thames are in for a rare treat.

You can charter this boat by day or by night, and we joined a party that did both. This way we were able to glean a wealth of historic information from the Captain about the famous sights on the riverbank, and later on enjoy cruising gently past the glittering lights of London reflected in the Thames.

The owner welcomed us aboard with a glass of sherry and the whole party was introduced to the crew by first names only, which made us feel instantly at home.

A particular feature of our cruise was the splendid medieval feast we were served

• • • • • • • • • •

by candlelight at the Captain's table. Here we enjoyed some unusual dishes: friar's feast, pyge in appul wyne and lech lombard. Each dish was explained to us by the Captain's wife, who had researched them all at London's riverside palaces; some of the dishes had been eaten by royalty as far back as 1215, when King John I was on the throne. After our feast we were served drinks and coffee on deck.

There is a comfortable lounge with green plants and brass fittings and a Victorian wood-burning stove. The woodwork is mahogany and the ceiling is quilted silk, an idea inspired by the ceiling in Queen Victoria's personal railway carriage. We admired the gleaming open-plan kitchen, where we could watch the chef preparing our meals. The well stocked bar stays open as long as the guests wish it to, and before we retired for the night we were invited to place our orders for early morning tea or coffee in bed.

All the cabins have en suite facilities and comfortable built-in beds of normal proportions. We had a prettily papered room that afforded ample accommodation with hanging space and a chest of drawers. Each cabin is named after a different lock: we noticed Sunbury, Shepperton and Old Windsor.

In the morning we enjoyed an enormous English breakfast while cruising past

beautiful Kew Gardens. The Captain invited us into the wheelhouse, and we were even given a chance to take the wheel, under his careful supervision.

Whether celebrating a private occasion or entertaining corporate clients, a stay aboard the Captain Webb can be recommended as an experience never to be forgotten.

• • • • • • • • • •

The Petersham Hotel

Nightingale Lane Richmond Surrey TW10 6UZ
Tel 081 940 7471 Fax 081 940 9998 Telex 928336 RGH G

54 rooms with bath and shower, telephone, tv, radio, hairdryer, mineral water (no mini bar or teasmade) • 24-hour room service, hot snacks between 7 a.m. and 10.45 p.m, English and Continental breakfast, laundry, dry cleaning • business services, safe, 3 meeting and private dining rooms • nearest restaurant: Nightingales (English and French) • lift, free parking • no animals • single room ££, double room ££–£££, suite ££, including breakfast, all major credit cards • tube and British Rail: Richmond; bus no: 65

Set in the lovely landscape of Richmond, The Petersham is an elegant Victorian building of considerable architectural significance. It was built as a hotel in 1865, and reflects the French and gothic style of the day. The architect was John Giles, who also designed The Langham Hotel in Westminster and Christ Church in Lambeth. The hotel underwent several changes of name, and was renamed The Petersham in 1978, after the nearby village and the surrounding meadows. The recent renovation of the building is totally in accord with the original design.

We stepped into the grand marble-floored foyer with its elegant reception area, and a friendly porter looked after our luggage while we enjoyed a drink in the traditionally furnished lounge, surrounded by oil paintings and antiques. Then we

• • • • • • • • • •

climbed the Portland stone staircase, which is claimed to be one of the longest unsupported central staircases in the country, admiring the remarkable ceiling paintings as we went. These were executed by Ferdinando Galli in 1865 and depict the painters Michelangelo, Titian, Raphael and Carracci.

Some of the luxury twin and double rooms offer four-poster beds, and many enjoy a panoramic view of the River Thames and the nearby rolling hills, the same view celebrated in oils by Turner and Reynolds.

The décor of the bedrooms perfectly combines the old and the new, and each is slightly different from the next. Most double rooms have a spacious corner bathtub and twin handbasins. Some have a separate sitting area. We admired the chintz bedspreads and curtains and appreciated the ample storage space.

Lunch in the hotel's restaurant, Nightingales, is something we will not easily forget, as the receptionist had reserved us a table right by the window overlooking the river. The view is breathtaking, and it is difficult to believe that the heart of London is only eight miles away.

In the evening we were treated to a totally different dining experience in The Cellar, where up to 20 guests can enjoy a candlelit dinner in the authentic atmosphere of a true working cellar. An iron and stone staircase led us down to where an astonishing 30,000 bottles of wine lie ageing along corridors under vaulted ceilings. The wine here has won such critical acclaim that the food is prepared to complement the wine and not vice versa.

During the day we visited Richmond Park, and were amazed to see deer roaming freely. This is a lovely place for a walk or a jog in the fresh air, and the hotel can also arrange for horse riding sessions.

The manager of The Petersham Hotel told us of its two sister hotels in France: Hôtel Château Tilques is near Saint-Omer and Hôtel Château Clarques (opening in 1994) is in the heart of the Pas-de-Calais. We hope to visit both.

• • • • • • • • •

The Richmond Gate Hotel

Richmond-upon-Thames Surrey TW10 6RP
Tel 081 940 0061 Fax 081 332 0354

**53 rooms with bath and shower, telephone, tv, radio, teasmade,
hairdryer, trouserpress, squash club, no air conditioning • room service
with hot and cold snacks from 5.30 to 11.00 p.m, full English and
Continental breakfast, laundry, dry cleaning • business services, safe,
5 conference rooms • in-house restaurant: Gates • free parking • no animals
• single room ££, double room ££, suite ££, including breakfast,
all major credit cards • tube: Richmond**

This hotel, situated at the top of Richmond Hill, was originally a collection of four
private eighteenth-century buildings, two cottages dating from 1728 and two
Georgian buildings from 1784. Each of these buildings has an interesting history.
They were converted into a hotel some 50 years ago and given the present name in
1968, after the neighbouring gate into Richmond Park. At this time a 44-room
extension was built at the back of the hotel, which also has a very attractive walled
garden and a herb garden used by the chef.

Eight more executive rooms will be finished by early 1993. The manager
informed us that they will feature antique furiture and traditional fabrics in yellow,
peach and blue. The bathrooms will have large corner tubs.

• • • • • • • • • •

The rooms in the extension are smaller and more modern in design, with one wall exposed to reveal the original brick. The furniture is in pine and the colour scheme pastel. By contrast, the bedrooms in the main body of the building are grand, elegant and traditional, with antique furniture in mahogany, maple, pine or oak. Some have four-poster beds. The bay windows allowed us a romantic view across the River Thames. The bathrooms are extremely large and well equipped with luxurious double washbasins.

We strolled around the magnificent garden before dinner. It is sometimes used for a private party or a barbecue in summer, and is perfect for an evening apéritif. The restaurant, Gates, is decorated in soft peach and furnished in cane; this light, bright room really has the power to lift the spirits. The menu is called Pride of Britain and offers traditional fare with a special line in puddings, and even British wines. The hotel buys the whole stock from a vineyard in Kent, so of course these exclusive wines cannot be found elsewhere.

After dinner we enjoyed a liqueur in the bar. The comfortable cane furniture is upholstered in burnt orange and vases of fresh flowers stand on glass-topped pine tables. There is a more mellow atmosphere in the club lounge, with its traditional leather chesterfields and armchairs.

We were only a few miles from the centre of London, but we could have been deep in the country. The hotel arranges for horse riding in Richmond Park, which made us think it would be perfect for a weekend break.

52 Mount Park Road

London W5 2BU
Tel 081 997 2243 Fax 081 997 4442

**2 rooms with en suite bath and shower, telephone (but not in room),
television, radio on request, teasmade, hairdryer, trouserpress,
complimentary chocolates and toiletries, no air conditioning • room
service, hot and cold snacks (no mini bar), English breakfast, laundry
(no dry cleaning) • conference room on request • in-house dinner can be
arranged • free parking • no animals • single room £, double room £,
credit cards: Amex, Visa, Access • closed over Christmas • tube and
mainline station: Ealing Broadway**

52 Mount Park Road is a Victorian villa in a quiet tree-lined avenue in Ealing,
West London. It is a very unusual hotel in that it has only two bedrooms, so
booking is essential. It is run by the owners, Paddy and Judith O'Hagan, who have
restored this once dilapidated double-fronted house to its former glory. Paddy, a
member of the original cast of *The Rocky Horror Show,* is now doing research at
London University; Judith's second home was The Dorchester Hotel in Park Lane,
built by her grandfather, who was its chairman for many years.

Judith and Paddy welcome guests as friends of the family, and every attention
was lavished on us during our stay. The house was crammed with interesting
artefacts and bric-à-brac, and we had the feeling of being in an old curiosity shop.

• • • • • • • • •

The twin bedrooms are truly Victorian in spirit as well as in furnishing. Among the knick-knacks we found complimentary boxes of biscuits and peppermints, and unusual teas and coffee to brew in the room. There was bottled mineral water at the bedside. The bathrooms have power showers and are well equipped with generous bottles of shampoo, bath and shower gel, and toothbrushes for forgetful guests.

We ate breakfast in the bright conservatory with its huge wicker sofas, comfortable cushions and a lovely view over the garden. Judith is an excellent cook. At breakfast she offered homemade jams and wholemeal bread, freshly ground coffee, prunes and freshly pressed fruit juice. She will also prepare dinner on request. The dining room also features interesting Victoriana. We spotted lovely tapestries and rugs sewn by Judith's mother, an old apothecary's chest, and dried flowers from the garden.

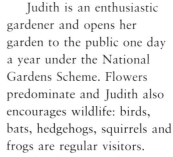

Judith is an enthusiastic gardener and opens her garden to the public one day a year under the National Gardens Scheme. Flowers predominate and Judith also encourages wildlife: birds, bats, hedgehogs, squirrels and frogs are regular visitors.

This fascinating house is conveniently situated for Kew Gardens, Heathrow Airport, Windsor Castle and, of course, central London.

• • • • • • • • •

The Edwardian International

Bath Road Hayes Middlesex UB3 5AW
Tel 081 897 6644 Fax 081 759 8422

459 air-conditioned rooms with bath and shower, telephone, answer machine, private fax, satellite tv with CNN, Sky, in-house movies; radio, mini bar (no teasmade), hairdryer, trouserpress, bathrobes • 24-hour room service, hot and cold snacks, English and Continental breakfast, laundry, dry cleaning, hairdressing, health club, swimming pool • business services, safe, 9 conference rooms • in-house restaurants: Henleys (British), The Brasserie (French) • lifts, free parking, shuttle service to and from airport • no animals • single room £££, double room £££, suite £££, breakfast not included, all major credit cards • nearest transport: Heathrow

No more cold lobbies, characterless bedrooms and poor restaurants: this is an airport hotel with everything to offer, in both style and facilities. The Edwardian International is only a few minutes by car from Heathrow. Once through the automatic doors, the jaded traveller is received into a world of comfort and luxury. The splendid lobby is floored in shimmering Italian marble, its walls are panelled in tropical kevasingo wood, and the ornate corniced ceiling is hung with a chandelier that comprises 20,000 individually cut crystals.

•••••••••

We checked into our fully air-conditioned room to find hand-decorated satinwood furniture, luxurious hangings and a window treatment designed to provide complete protection from the airport lights. The windows throughout the hotel are hermetically sealed to guarantee a peaceful night. Guest rooms are equipped with a unique telephone system. By punching in a code when leaving the room, we were able to arrange for a personal answering service. Besides the usual television channels, we could also watch in-house movies and German, French and Italian satellite programmes.

Though all the bedrooms have a separate bathroom, the 17 suites also have a lounge and a whirlpool spa bath, and some have four-poster beds, bidets, steam showers and separate WCs.

The business facilities are without parallel. A nine-suite convention centre takes up to 750 delegates in the County Suite. Here we found yew-panelled walls, crystal chandeliers, and deep pile handmade carpets of pure wool from the Orient. Conferences can be videoed and recorded or relayed live to the delegates' bedrooms.

However, the main attraction for the tourist has to be the Pegasus Health Spa and poolside terrace. Enclosed within a glass atrium, the terrace overlooks the swimming pool. Interesting features include a landscaped waterfall, York stone walkways and a koi carp pool. The health spa has a gymnasium, sauna and massage rooms, and beauty and hairdressing salons.

Adjoining the poolside terrace is The Brasserie. Breakfast can be served here, on the terrace or in your room. The Polo Lounge next door has a colonial atmosphere. More tropical hardwoods panel the walls and the seats of the bar stools are leather saddles. The deep sofas in the Henley Lounge invite you to relax over cocktails before dinner in the Henley Restaurant, with its traditional English cuisine featuring organic vegetables, and extensive and extravagant wine list.

The Edwardian International contains a number of shops, including Burberrys, a newsagent, a travel agent, a jeweller, and a country gifts shop.

The authors and publisher would like to thank all those hotels who kindly supplied pictures for this book, and also photographers **Brian Cohen** (front jacket, back jacket top and bottom left and top right, 18-19, 30-31, 34-35, 42-49, 54-55, 56-57, 60-61, 66-67, 72 bottom, 74-75, 82-83, 92-93, 100-101, 106-107, 108-109, 116-117, 120-121, 122-123, 140, 146, 148-149, 154-155, 162-163, 164-165, 166-167, 182-183, 188-189), **Neill Menneer** (half title verso, 8, 10 top and bottom, 26, 27, 28 top and bottom, 70, 72 top, 88, 89, 90 top and bottom, 113, 114, 136, 137, 138, 150, 151, 152 top and bottom, 158, 160, 177, 178), **Andrew Lawson** (112, 159) and **Michael Dent** (176), and designer **Kelly j Maskall** (maps 11, 29, 53, 73, 91, 115, 139, 161, 179).

• • • • • • • • • •